THE
ULTIMATE STEP

THE
ULTIMATE STEP

Dr. T. Logan Smith

Alpharetta, GA

Although the author has made every effort to ensure that the information in this book was correct at press time and while this publication is designed to provide accurate information in regard to the subject matter covered, the author assumes no responsibility for errors, inaccuracies, omissions, or any other inconsistencies herein and hereby disclaims any liability to any party for any loss, damage, or disruption caused by errors or omissions, whether such errors or omissions result from negligence, accident, or any other cause. Limited masking of names and details was utilized to protect the anonymity of individuals and their families. The author disclaims any liabilities in connection to the use of this information.

Copyright © 2020 by Dr. Logan Smith

All rights reserved. No part of this book may be reproduced or transmitted in any form or by any means, electronic or mechanical, including photocopying, recording, or any information storage and retrieval system, without permission in writing from the author.

ISBN: 978-1-63183-972-6 - Paperback
ISBN: 978-1-63183-973-3 - Hardcover
eISBN: 978-1-63183-974-0 - ePub
eISBN: 978-1-63183-975-7 - Mobi

ISBNs are the property of Heavenly Light Press for the express purpose of sales and distribution of this title. The content of this book is the property of the copyright holder only. Heavenly Light Press does not hold any ownership of the content of this book and is not liable in any way for the materials contained within. The views and opinions expressed in this book are the property of the Author/Copyright holder, and do not necessarily reflect those of Heavenly Light Press.

Printed in the United States of America   1 1 2 4 2 0

♾ This paper meets the requirements of ANSI/NISO Z39.48-1992 (Permanence of Paper)

*In memory of and gratitude for the life
of my dear brother Dr. Solomon Abegunde
who inspired me never to quit, but persevere in faith,
service, and gratitude to our Lord Jesus Christ*

Contents

Preface ix
Author's Introduction: "Let's Talk" xi

PART ONE: REMEMBERING

Chapter 1: Bud Kendrick 3
Chapter 2: Charles Castellaw 19
Chapter 3: Nana 31
Chapter 4: Sis 45
Chapter 5: Old Joe 59
Chapter 6: Kay 75
Chapter 7: George Edwards 89
Chapter 8: John 105

PART TWO: ANTICIPATING

Chapter 9: Two Irrefutable Conclusions 135
Chapter 10: The Affirmation of the Old Testament 151
Chapter 11: The Affirmation of the New Testament 179
Chapter 12: The Ultimate Step 197

Epilogue: Unfinished Business 215
Appendix A 223
Appendix B 225

Preface

This book has taken a career of research and reflection to write. Its purpose is to provide comfort and hope to the grieving amid the reality of death and to serve as a resource for others ministering to the grieving. The people whose stories are documented in this book are people I have known and loved. Only a few of the names are masked for the privacy of the families involved. Only one story is the blend of two families who faced almost identical situations and were blended for the same reason. All the visions and testimonies of the individuals facing death are exactly as I remember them with no literary liberties taken. My commitment to their exact words is uncompromised as my great concern is to stand no other but our Lord Jesus Christ as preeminent, loving, and faithful. May He alone be the focus of every reading of this book.

Author's Introduction
"Let's Talk"

Ironically, it was his final role. I refer to the late John Wayne's portrayal of John Bernard "J.B." Books in the movie western entitled "The Shootist." The movie was filmed in 1976, one year following the publication of the novel "The Shootist" written by Glendon Swarthout, upon which its storyline was based.

According to the plot, the events occur in January of 1901 in Carson City, Nevada. J. B. Books is the last of the famous men of the old west who lives by his gun. His reputation as a gunslinger who has killed numerous men is unparalleled. "All deserved it," He said.

But he has come to Nevada City at this time, not to take another man's life, but to face the end of his own. He has cancer. His remaining days are few. Each remaining day is mentally and physically torturous. Every day his doctor's prognosis of an excruciating, painful death is proving to be true as he incessantly drinks laudanum to kill the increasing pain.

Mentally his grief relating to his own mortality is compounded by the fact that he is alone and feeling lonely to the very depths of his soul. In fact, in all of Carson City, Books has few, if any, friends. One friendly voice is the owner of the local livery stable with whom he "haggles" to sell his only real assets apart from his pistol: his horse and saddle. Another friendly voice is that of his physician who passively suggests that Books end his own life immediately rather than face the inevitable pain and agony of his cancerous death.

When he arrives in Carson City, initially he attempts to keep both his identity and his illness a secret. He knows that his presence is unwanted. He also is aware that if another person learns of his illness, given his reputation, that person would likely seek to take advantage of his illness for his or her own personal benefit. These realities only enhance the fact that he is not only alone, but desperately lonely.

Given his situation, he rents a room in a boarding house owned and operated by the widow Bond Rogers and Gillom, her teenage son. He registers under a false name. Here he plans to die.

However, his identity is soon discovered. Mrs. Rogers is both frightened and infuriated. She summons the local sheriff who orders Books to leave town. The sheriff withdraws his order only after Books reveals that his death is imminent, which eventually leads to a most poignant moment of confrontation between Mrs. Rogers and J. B. Books.

That is when Books completely bears his soul in one single statement. He says to Mrs. Rogers summing up his refusal to leave, "I'm a dying man, scared of the dark!"

The scene is ironic, given that John Wayne is portraying J. B. Books. For years earlier, John Wayne, himself, had been diagnosed with lung cancer with a bleak prognosis. But after the surgical removal of one lung and several ribs, he miraculously recovered and was clinically declared to be cancer free. His recovery was so dramatic that he was able to return to his acting profession for additional years of creative success in various western roles.

But little did he know that "The Shootist" would be his last role. For not long after the completion of the film, it was discovered that he again had cancer. As a result, he would die within months of that diagnosis.

When he said, portraying J. B. Books, who had been diagnosed with terminal cancer, "I'm a dying man, scared of the dark," he had no idea how imminent due to cancer his own death was! Was John Wayne afraid of the dark? I do not know. I have been told that John Wayne became a Christian before his death. But in truth, I believe that most men and women are afraid of the dark, especially when it comes to their own mortality.

That is why I am writing this book. That is why it is my desire for you, the reader, with me to approach this subject. I am convinced that there is a little of J. B. Books in all of us. However, I do not wish to address the subject "generally speaking;" rather it is my desire to do so from a "distinctively Christian" point of view.

This book is focused on the Christian experience of death. Within its pages I will explore specific questions regarding the death experience of a Christian that I have been asked repeatedly throughout my career as a vocational minister. These questions include: How might one define the death experience of a Christian? What happens at the moment of a Christian's death? What does a Christian person feel? What does a Christian person know? What does a Christian person see? What does a Christian person hear?

Many critics assert that no one knows the answers to these questions and other related questions, nor can they know. They present as their primary argument the idea that no one has returned to life after experiencing a certain death. Of course, I must concede their point except for one glaring exception: Jesus did! I believe that Jesus did return to life after experiencing death not only because of His own testimony, the Biblical revelation and the existential experience of affirmed faith; but I also believe that Jesus returned to life after experiencing death because of the tangible, physical evidence that would stand the litmus test of any modern court of law. Such evidence is the subject of another book, time, and space.

These same critics often further fail to acknowledge perhaps the most striking additional evidence we are given as to what happens at the moment of death: namely, the testimony of the men and women who are actually experiencing that moment of transition.

For over forty years I have held the hands of men and women, and yes, even boys and girls, as they described to me their visions and sensations during those final moments before breathing their last earthly breath.

As I have catalogued a number of these intimate moments, I have been most arrested by several findings. First, Christians simply do not die as others who are not of the Christian faith. There are unique visions and realizations that Christians experience in light of their faith. Second, varying social standings, levels of affluence, educational backgrounds, career choices, cultural lineages and other such sociological demarcations do not seem to result in any significant differences of insight or awareness for those Christian individuals amid their final moments before death. The experience of the death of a "Christian" entails an indisputable consistency. In every case study the visions, sensations, and awarenesses are remarkably similar. Third, there is the element of a "consistent surprise" that is so mysteriously wonderful that the dying individual then desires death so completely that ultimately anything less is unacceptable. This "surprise" is seemingly omnipresent.

As you read and contemplate a few of the examples I cite in this book-- which are only a random sampling of many similar experiences-- and as I share a number of my conclusions, you may recall others within your own experience you find meaningful. But whether or not you have witnessed such an occasion, I submit to you, the reader, that the testimony of the individuals I have cited in which they described their own death experience is a valid testimony of what actually happens in the life of every Christian at his or her moment of death.

One other critic up front must be given his due. I refer to the critic who ascribes such testimony to the chemical interactions within a dying brain. I have read numerous books on the subject. I have sat within numerous forums, listened to the arguments, and studied the findings of highly respected scholars who believe in the theory of progressive chemical death. My conclusion is that this view simply does not stand up to the evidence that a Christian's death is a unique experience, much less a desired one. Many fine Christian medical apologists have diffused such critics who attempt to explain away a dying individual's experience of visions and epiphany. All such debate I also leave to another time and place.

So back to where I began. What happens to a Christian at the moment of death? What is unique to the Christian himself or herself at the moment of death? What is unique to the Christian's overall death experience? In the following chapters I share only an abbreviated description of my journey as I have participated with numerous Christian friends, family, and others in their death experiences.

Now I would be remiss if I did not express a genuine debt of gratitude to a number of individuals who have contributed to the writing of this book. Foremost is my wife, Carol, who has shared forty-nine years of marriage with me. Her love and support are and have been my stalwarts. My dear children (and I do not have "in-laws" just additional children), Bryant, BethAnn, Joe, and Ashley are deep wells of fresh motivation, love, and inspiration. My two dear grandsons, Smith and Bo, are my pride, joy, and hope. Their unconditional love, confidence and trust ignite within me the courage of conviction.

The individuals and families of the deceased whose stories I share with their permission, but in some cases using assumed names, are to be greatly thanked and praised for their encouragement to both me, the writer, and you, the reader, and their courage in allowing their stories to be told.

The numerous others involved in the actual production of the text (e.g. typists, editors, redactors) have all been superb in their roles and are also to be thanked. To each I express my deepest thanks!

But words alone will never adequately express my deepest gratitude to a few individuals for their inspiration, encouragement, and assistance. Without them, this book would never have been completed. Rosy and Henry Brown, John Foster, Wink Verdery, Emory Jones, and Phil Hudgins are gifts from God to me.

What happens at the moment of death? Let's listen in.

Part One
Remembering

*Depend on it, your dying moment
will be the best hour you have ever known!*

— C. H. Spurgeon

Chapter 1

Bud Kendrick

I cannot remember from my childhood my first awareness of death. Perhaps the reason is because my parents chose never to insulate me as a child from the reality of death. Born in the early 1950's, I found the images of death as numerous as the experiences were varied.

For example, my earliest images include the "wakes" associated with funerals held in private homes. I recall the scurried activities of the wake that included the preparing for the coffin containing the body of the beloved deceased to be brought into the home, whereupon it was displayed for viewing by the public who would drop by to express sympathies, weep with the bereaved, communicate in whispered conversation, and sit in silence, all to support the grieved. Most of the guests brought "covered dishes" which resulted in the sharing of platters and bowls of food for both the grieved and the supportive guests.

I recall rare, very rare occasions being allowed in "the back room" where the nearest of kin, particularly the spouse or parents of the deceased, stayed almost in incubation in order to weep and grieve openly, but usually only in the presence of one or two others.

If the family of the deceased was affluent, I remember the family and friends going to the funeral home uptown where everything was more "public." And too, uptown there were flowers of every color, fragrance, and genre, many of which everyone knew did not grow locally and were only seen at funerals or weddings. The flowers were all prepared by local florists. The florist of choice was often the preacher's wife who had an extraordinary talent for incorporating ribbons, ferns, portraits, family momenta, Bible verses and other items such as plastic telephones with the declaration "Jesus called" into the floral arrangements.

I recall quite vividly the actual funerals. It was not uncommon for three, four or five ministers to give a eulogy or on occasion an "evangelistic sermon," although as a child I did not know the difference; and, based on my observation, many of the ministers I have heard even to this day still do not know the difference.

I recall at the funerals themselves, after two hours or longer of sitting and listening to the ministers' remarks and sermons, exiting the church or chapel to walk toward the cemetery in a "processional," as my parents would call it; or getting into the car to drive to the cemetery (not even the preacher knew the word "cortege" in those days), whereupon arriving we walked "in a proper pecking order" to the grave site and stood, as the family sat, only to listen again to the preachers repeat everything they had said indoors. Finally, after all the climatic remarks were made and the longest prayer of the whole service was uttered, everybody shook hands, laughed, stood around and talked. As a child I never knew whether they were simply glad to see each other again or just overjoyed that the service was over.

But this much even as a child I knew. The person who had died was gone. And when it was a member of the family, I knew they were loved and missed. But reflecting, I do not ever recall at the funeral, wake or elsewhere, anyone talking about the deceased's moment of death unless it was a description of an accident, health issue, or "untimely" event. No one to my memory discussed the actual moment of death except perhaps briefly, using pastoral metaphors such as "home going," "crossing over" as in crossing rivers or oceans, or "transformation" as in God needing another angel.

I do not recall the issue of the reality of the moment of death being discussed. No one inquired as to what the deceased acknowledged, experienced, or envisioned. The closest anyone to my memory came to the subject without speaking in metaphor-- and I write with no disrespect intended-- was in the case of a convicted capitol crime offender being executed via the electric chair in Jackson, Georgia, whereupon public curiosity never failed to ask, "What were his last words?"…words usually published the next day in various newspapers. So even as a child, death was real and its images, many of which exist to this day, were familiar.

However, these images eventually would be proven limited and my perceptions of death would be enlarged and challenged. And questions regarding the moment of death would, as others might say it, appear suddenly on my radar.

The year it first happened was 1970. I was 18 years of age and a freshman at Norman Junior College, located in the small hamlet of Norman Park near Moultrie, Georgia. My life was rather uncomplicated and narrowly structured.

My stack poles of concern and focus were: the love of my life, Carol; basketball, which financed my education; making the grade academically in light of a possible future career as an architect; and addressing those existential "religious" questions consistent with late adolescence-- all in that order.

Of course, there was my family. Mother, dad, four younger siblings, a live-in maternal grandmother, a "live outside in her mobile home" paternal grandmother, a pet or two, and a host of aunts and uncles and cousins always kept my life from getting too boring, stale or uncomplicated. Anyone from a large family understands both the wit and realism of such a circumstance.

As it was with large families, particularly extended families, there were always relatives of every category and description. There were those relatives you saw rarely. Others of them you saw frequently. Some you adored. Others you questioned their DNA. Some you rushed to embrace. Others you saw coming and from them, as a child particularly, you attempted to hide to avoid that suffocating squeeze and sloppy kiss, most prominently at what once was hallowed "family reunions."

Within my extended family there was more than one uncle and aunt to whom I felt extremely close. Each made a significant contribution to my growth and development for which I am eternally grateful. Each I loved in a unique way. Each, I knew beyond any question, loved me in return.

Not one among them, for the purpose of this writing, had a greater influence upon me than "Uncle Bud." His given name was Henry Alexander Kendrick. But I have an idea that very few people except my aunt, his physicians, employer, and the IRS ever knew him by that name. I must admit that until I read his tombstone, I did not know his full name. He was simply, "Uncle Bud" … to others "Bud" … to a few "Mr. Kendrick."

His simple name "Uncle Bud" was itself a genuine porthole

into the reality of the man. His life and world were simple. Faith, family, and work would succinctly describe his prioritized world; a wise ordering of priorities for any individual, I am convinced, even to this day.

As others in the family tell me, Uncle Bud never traveled far, literally, or metaphorically speaking, from the day or station of his birth. He was born in 1908, which itself lends insight into his moorings. He was born into a lower, middle class family, or as others might describe it, upper poverty level family. But although money was scarce, the virtues of personal dignity, honesty, hard work and a simple Biblical faith were not.

Uncle Bud was the epitome of the "Norman Rockwell Granddad." He stood about 6'6" tall. Kendrick men are to this day still noted for their height. Uncle Bud was no exception. But apart from his physical stature, Uncle Bud stood tall in a myriad of complementary ways.

For example, he was a knowledgeable man. One might think otherwise if he or she were told that Uncle Bud's formal education never exceeded the fifth grade, which is true. But Uncle Bud's education was gleaned more through sweat and determination than textbook and pen…remember there were no computers in those days.

For example, he learned to utilize his large hands, and all of us who loved him remember those large hands, to fabricate and repair machinery. His skills applied to any machine of the day that I can remember.

His official vocational title was that of "head maintenance man" for the Dundee Mills plant number five of Griffin, Georgia. Dundee Mills was a textile firm known for producing primarily terry towels of every variety. Plant number five was a grey mill, meaning it produced a towel from the initial bale of cotton to its "pre-finishing" state right off the loom. Uncle Bud made that happen.

In return, he was paid a modest salary and afforded a four-room house in the mill village of crowded similar houses. They were simple, but comfortable although by today's standards some might regard Uncle Bud's house as crude, most likely because originally it had only a one-seat outhouse out back. Why even in the country as a boy I remember our family had a two-seater although I cannot remember over one seat ever being used at a time.

But Uncle Bud's one-seater is vivid in my mind still sixty years later most likely because that is where Uncle Bud caught me and a friend, Chester Foster, as young boys trying out our first Camel cigarettes that Chester had absconded from his father.

And in spite of the fact that smoking in those days was something of a males' rise to status--after all it was the day of the Marlboro Man who I believe even my dad tried to emulate to the day of his cancerous death--Uncle Bud was not impressed by the Marlboro man or by the "foul odor" of others who did. He made that very clear to me.

So being caught in his outhouse taking my first and last draw on any cigarette, I expected him to painfully discipline me. That practice called spanking, switching, or whooping, was popular then, and effective. I cannot help sometimes but wonder if, with moderation, we might have lost something in that area…oh yes, another day. Another book.

But on that occasion Uncle Bud did not take to the disciplining rod, nor did he scream or scold. Rather, he reached out that large hand of his, placed it on my shoulder, stooped to one knee, looked me squarely in the eye and spoke with words laced with momentary disappointment but unmistakable and unshakable love. And although I cannot remember verbatim his words, his message is still indelibly etched in my mind, "Son, you are better than this. You do not need a foul-smelling cigarette in your mouth to be a man. You have a mind and a body worth keeping clean. Hiding in outhouses or anywhere else is beneath you if you are honest and doing what is right. Smoking is unnecessary and not the best for you. I want the best for you. I want you to want the best too. Please let this be the end of this…just between you and me…okay?"

That was the last cigarette I ever put to my lips. I knew Uncle Bud was right. Now that I am older, I would call him wise. If a one-seater could ever become an altar, I suppose it was that day for me.

So, Uncle Bud's simple house in the mill village, call it comfortable or crude, was itself a special place. Because of what among many other things I learned there, I will just call it sacred. It was a special day when Dundee Mills allowed Uncle Bud no longer to lease, but to purchase the house and property. It was perhaps the single greatest physical asset Uncle Bud ever owned.

But as evidenced by the account of being disciplined I have just described, Uncle Bud was not only knowledgeable vocationally, in addition he had a love for people. I could never categorize him as outgoing nor include him in today's stereotype of a people person, but his friends and family knew it, especially we children.

His love for us children was no doubt to a great extent formed within the painful forge and upon the agonizing anvil of his own great grief. You see, Uncle Bud had only two biological children of his own, both died in early infancy.

And though their deaths left a gaping hole in his heart, he allowed us children to play there, learn there, love him there and grow there.

Some people might have said that Uncle Bud was never happier than when, dressed in his trademark flannel shirt and overalls, he was out and among his animals he deeply loved…a varied herd I recall of two cows he taught us to milk by hand (he had no modern machinery in those days), one horse he allowed us boys to ride, one rare goat nobody bothered, and only a couple of chickens for an egg here and there.

But as "at home" as Uncle Bud seemed among his animals, I never knew him to be happier than when he was among us children…a gentle giant teaching us various things which at the time we did not realize would be invaluable to us later. For example, I never go fishing to this day, a pastime I greatly enjoy, without thinking of him. I still use the simple fisherman's knot he taught me to tie. And his words have yet to be disapproved: "Tie this knot carefully and correctly, and it will not ever fail you and cost you a catch." Oh yes, my favorite fishing partner, my grandson, uses that same knot today.

Uncle Bud was genuine, most knowledgeable, loving, and forthright with us children in other areas of his life. The most important area, unquestionably, was that of his Christian faith. It was never a secret to us kids that Uncle Bud wanted us to share his Christian faith.

He communicated that fact without lecturing or sermonizing.

If Uncle Bud ever proved himself in any formal way of being capable of preaching a sermon or lecturing in front of a Sunday School classroom, I am not aware of it. But he taught us children and we learned, nevertheless. Although I do not ever remember him quoting it or expounding upon it, I do recall that large hand on my shoulder in cadence with his gentle voice saying, "Just remember John 3:16 son…Just remember John 3:16." He believed it. He wanted us to believe it too.

But make no mistake, Uncle Bud did attend the little East Griffin Baptist Church at least once most Sundays. He did contribute a tithe as best he could.

But he was not within the common power circles, theological quarrels, para-church activities or other highly visible "movers, shakers, and drivers" of the little congregation. He left all that "churchmanship" to others.

Again, he was just the simple, gentle, tall but almost otherwise unnoticed man, unless something mechanically broke, who appeared with a degree of consistency to sing, pray and remind the children, "Remember John 3:16…son, daughter (then a smile) John 3:16."

One other aspect of this relationship between Uncle Bud and us children must be underscored. As we children aged, our relationship with Uncle Bud matured and became stronger as well.

I have heard many adults bewail the distancing of their relationships with their children, saying things such as, "When the kids achieved high school, I turned around and they were gone," or, "One day I looked and asked, 'Where did the kids go?' and nobody knew."

It was not that way with Uncle Bud. We grew with him

together. His ability to do so with us was perhaps one of his strongest heavenly spiritual gifts.

So, I return to the one date I have already mentioned ... The year it first happened that my perceptions of death and life after death would be critically and wonderfully challenged and enlarged; and most importantly, the question of, "What happens at the moment of one's death?" appeared on my radar.

It was the fall of 1970, more specifically, Friday, October 8, late afternoon, Uncle Bud's dinnertime; but he never called it dinnertime, it was suppertime.

The place was the Griffin-Spalding County Hospital, a fine, progressive medical facility with an excellent team of physicians, nurses and support staff that provided care second to none for Spalding County and the surrounding counties located due south of Atlanta and north of Macon along the still relatively new Interstate 75 corridor.

Uncle Bud had been recently in and out of the hospital, but recently more in than out. He had been suffering from a condition known as asthmatic breathing likely due to his years in the grey mill.

On this occasion of his hospitalization, like numerous others, it was not believed that his problems were immediately life threatening, not in the least. In fact, on this Friday evening it was believed that he would be released the first thing in the morning to return home to resume his daily routine.

I was preparing to return from my home in Orchard Hill, Georgia, a small hamlet five miles south of Griffin, to Norman College some two-and-a-half hours to three hours away toward the Florida line, when the idea arose that I would like to visit Uncle Bud for a few minutes.

I knew that I would not be able to return home again for some time due to the formal beginning of the basketball season. In fact, this very night a "Midnight Madness" scrimmage would be held along with a massive pep rally including the press to kick-off the season.

Being a scholarship player, projected starter, and the touted " new boy come to town," there was no question as to my being there and remaining almost confined to the campus for the next few months with the exception of away games, Thanksgiving and Christmas tournaments, and the play-offs of course.

So, the decision was almost as instantaneous as the idea to swing by the hospital to enjoy a few minutes with Uncle Bud. Frankly, I was a bit surprised to find him, not in his hospital bed, but dressed in his bath robe and pajamas sitting in the corner chair of his room usually only occupied by a visitor.

Furthermore, he was reading a book, something frankly I had never witnessed him doing. I knew he could read. I had seen him browsing a newspaper, but I had never seen a book other than his Bible in his hand. I regret to this day, that I did not inquire as to the title or genre of the book. I can only wonder.

But as I entered the room, he closed the book and rested it on his lap. I leaned over him with that somewhat awkward but familiar embrace of our greeting. I said as one might expect, "Uncle Bud, you are looking great. I am glad you are doing so much better!"

I can still see upon the screen of my mind that good old boy country grin on his face as he said, "I am fine son. I'm just fine."

We engaged in further small talk. Noticing the clock that hung on the wall at the foot of his bed, I felt compelled to say, "Well,

Uncle Bud, I wish I had more time, but I must hit the road. I not only must get to the campus and get unpacked; I must get to the gym, get dressed and begin participating in the Midnight Madness shoot around before the coach ever arrives on the court. If I am given the opportunity to make a quick visit home any time soon, I will be certain to come by and see you."

That is when it happened. A two-tier conversation began without my full awareness. It would be one that I would not understand for some time later, and more fully not until years later.

Uncle Bud said, still grinning but with an immediate gravity in his voice, "No son, you will not see me. I will not be here."

Thinking that he was referring to the hospital with something of his dry sense of humor, I said, "I know you will not be here. I know you are going home in the morning. I mean, I will come by your house to see you. I hope you will be through with hospitals for a while."

Said he, "No, son, you do not understand. I am sharing with you that I will not be back in East Griffin either. And I am through with hospitals."

Still not understanding, I replied, "Uncle Bud, wherever you are I will find you."

He almost chuckled, though still gravely serious. He said, "No, son. You will not find me. Today I had a heavenly visitor. I received my long distant telephone call. I am going…" and with a wide smile, a slow swallow and a deep breath he paused, then added, "Home. I am going with Jesus to my heavenly home. I will not be here in the morning. A lot of folks will not understand that everything is okay, and I am fine. But it is! I am and I will be just fine. You will understand."

At that moment, if there was ever an eighteen-year old boy with a thick skull and a dim ability to see, it was me. I confess, with some regret, I still did not get it. I did not grasp what Uncle Bud was trying to fully communicate to me.

I expressed my goodbye again with another light embrace. The only thought I can recall pondering was, "Well Uncle Bud, wherever your home is located, or 'new home' is located, I will find you."

Several hours later, with little time to spare, but time enough, I reported to the campus gymnasium. Our special uniforms for the Midnight Madness were already hanging in our lockers. The only thing that seemed out of step with the moment was that on my jersey the anticipated and promised number 31 had been for some reason supplanted by the number 45, but that seemed of little consequence, and it was.

I dressed and reported to the basketball court for the shoot around, thankful that I was neither the first nor the last player to do so, and even more thankful that the coach had yet to make his entrance.

As a sports broadcaster might describe it, I had mentally just begun to get into "the zone", and even the more difficult shots had begun to fall when one of the team trainers came onto the basketball court, tapped me on the shoulder and said, "Logan, the coach is still in his office and he wants to see you now."

Somewhat startled out of "my zone" and a little shaken by "the coach wants to see you now," I immediately tossed aside the basketball I was holding and made my way to his office nearby. Along the way I simply could not fathom, "What have I done to be called into the coach's office, especially now? Surely, I had not missed any date or time to which I or the team had been obligated. What possibly could a private meeting with the coach less than a half-hour before tip-off actually concern?"

When I entered the office, I first noticed that the coach seemed himself a bit uneasy, which only added to my immediate anxiety. Coach Ruark was always anything but uneasy. He stood about 5'10" tall. He had the build of a football linebacker. His slightly graying, almost military haircut added to his intimidation factor. I always thought he favored the immortal Vince Lombardi, without the hat.

My perception of his ill at ease somewhat permeated the room. "Sit down," he said as he walked over to me and did something he never had done. He put his hand on my shoulder in Uncle Bud fashion and said, "Son, I have some sad news for you. At first I thought I might keep it from you until after tonight's game.

"But then I thought… no. You will be starting for us and we both know that. You are in shape and ready to go. No doubt about that. And tonight, as important as it is for the public, is not really going to significantly impact our team.

"Logan you have an uncle to whom you are close named, Bud, do you not?"

"I do!"

"Well, Logan, I am sorry to tell you that earlier this evening, as a patient at the hospital in Griffin, he unexpectedly passed away. I want you to go home now, be with your family, and be back at practice on Tuesday, which will allow time for the funeral. This way when you return to the campus, I know you will be ready to go."

The Ultimate Step

I thanked the coach for his genuine concern. As I returned to the dressing room, I remember thinking even now, fifty years later, "Now I know. Now I understand what Uncle Bud was trying to help me comprehend. John 3:16 was no longer for him a mere promise, but a certain reality. And he knew. He knew that within literally minutes of our saying goodbye… less than an hour…he was indeed as his heavenly visitor had told him, going home, to his eternal, heavenly home. And he had that peace of which our Lord spoke when he described the peace that passes all understanding, 'my peace' (see John 14), whereby he could say to me with the deepest of sincerity, "I'm fine. And it's going to be okay."

Although at the time, it would not be an in depth or prolonged contemplation as years later it would become, I remember thinking as I drove in the wee hours of that night from Norman Park back to Griffin, "He knew he was leaving this world, that his death was imminent. He knew because as he had testified, 'I had a visitation…I received my long distant telephone call.'"

"What visitation? Who visited him? Who had told him, infusing both courage and confidence, that he was drawing his final breath? No doubt he had seen something or someone. No doubt he had heard and knew to be true whatever he had been told."

Following Uncle Bud's funeral, I immediately returned to the college campus with both its academic and athletic responsibilities. Although Uncle Bud would be deeply missed these questions about "his visitation" would admittedly quickly fade. For as a typical college freshman, the matters of the human and divine Spirit did not occupy a priority focus.

But this whole matter of a "visitation" at the moment of death would emerge again. Not immediately, but following several years and a lifestyle change later, another man dear to my heart would ask, "Don't you see?"

Chapter 2

Charles Castellaw

"How quickly time passes" is more than a cliché. The year was 1981. In the eleven years since the death of my Uncle Bud (Kendrick) I had experienced more than a few major life transitions.

For example, I was no longer the single guy in college still dating his high school sweetheart. Rather, I was the husband of Carol, my high school sweetheart, and the proud father of two children. My young son, Bryant, was the older, followed by our daughter, BethAnn, only twenty-one months the younger.

Additionally, I had experienced significant career changes. After two years of college I had entered the work force as a minor partner in my father's complete car care and service business.

But I quickly learned that though blood may be thicker than water it is not always an effective epoxy for a healthy working environment amid different opinions or visions. Without any injury to family relationships, and coupled with further education, I returned my corporate stock in the family business to my father and became employed as an industrial engineer by Dundee Mills of Griffin, Georgia. Frankly, for several years I tremendously enjoyed and profited from that textile career. I believe I could have enjoyed it to this day.

However, following a personal, spiritual epiphany of religious experience, tearfully and yet confidently obedient to that epiphany, I resigned my textile career to yet again return to college and theological graduate school following which I accepted the pastorate of the Calvary Baptist Church in Griffin, Georgia.

That was my position in 1981. I was a full time Baptist minister and senior pastor while in the dissertation phase of my doctoral degree, which I completed not long thereafter.

That is when it happened. Today, as I reflect upon it, it was nothing less than another unique, divinely orchestrated encounter with a man I admired and loved as he left this world to encounter life-beyond through which I was given insight into the death experience beyond "the norm," even for a minister.

Of course, as a minister, dealing with death was not an uncommon or uncomfortable experience for me. Painful, yes, but such separation always is. But grieving with those who grieved, both in anticipation of death, as well as following the death experience, given the size of my congregation, was almost a weekly experience. Writing funeral sermons and eulogies was reverently commonplace although never routine. The reality of death and its affects were never far away.

Nevertheless, not since the death of Uncle Bud and his sincere attempt to give me unusual insight into the death experience, had anything quite so illuminous occurred. And though my insight into the concept of death was quickened and deepened, perhaps the most dynamic revelation was this: as different as Uncle Bud and Mr. Charles were, their experiences were synonymous. They were identical.

This cherished episode began on a Thursday afternoon as I was traveling to Emory Hospital in Atlanta to visit a member of my church who had recently undergone surgery and thankfully was recovering well.

As I proceeded along Clairmont Road toward Emory Hospital, I noticed to my right the Veterans Hospital in Decatur, Georgia. Seeing the hospital, I recalled a conversation I had shared with my father earlier in the day in Griffin, Georgia. In that conversation he had mentioned that Mr. Charles Castellaw, who I had not seen in several years, was seriously ill and confined to his bed in the Veterans Hospital. My father had no idea of the actual nature or prognosis of his illness, but he thought I might like to know.

Of course, I did. You see, I had first met Mr. Charles when I was only a young boy growing up in Orchard Hill, Georgia. Mr. Charles was the husband of Mrs. Eloise. Mrs. Eloise was my Sunday school teacher, Vacation Bible School teacher, and overall, the second mother of all the children at the small countryside Rehoboth Baptist Church. Those facts alone made Mr. Charles important.

But even more significant to me was the fact that he was the father of my two best friends. Danny was an overall playmate and partner in crime. He was a year older than I, but that seemed not to matter. Maribeth, to this day a beautiful and marvelous person, was a classmate and the closet sister I ever had next to, and not far from, my siblings.

Through those developmental years of childhood and even adolescence, the Castellaw home was not just another house but a second home not far from my biological family home. Why, it was there with the Castellaw clan that I learned and had reinforced many important life lessons, not the least of which was the importance of church, family, faith, how to raise three days old calves on a bottle, pick cotton for a full day, ride a horse, shoot a gun, swim (in their pond), and play spin-the-bottle at birthday parties.

Mr. Charles, when he was at home, played a large role in many of these lessons. And I say, "when he was at home" because in the earlier years, Mr. Charles was a career Navy man, a man who served honorably and well for twenty-eight years. It was always a joyous time when, prior to his retirement, Mr. Charles could have military leave to spend time at home.

It was following his retirement that I got to know him best. He was short in stature, compared to me, but he stood tall. The feature I remember about him most was not his balding head, which Danny would later perpetuate, but his endearing smile.

As I wrote his eulogy, I emphatically stated that he was faithful to his name. And he was! For Charles is "a strong name of Teutonic or ancient German origin, (which) translated means 'a man among people, a friend, a man that loves people.' (He) was indeed a man like that. He loved people…He always had a good word and a smile for his friends and his family."

That was Mr. Charles. Of course, as tender as his smile was, make no mistake about it, he was also U.S. Navy tough. Wonderfully, he had that rare gift of knowing when and where to be both…tough and tender.

Maybe that is why he was so effective as an employee in the Georgia State Penal System following his retirement from the military. You see, he hung up his naval uniform in 1973. But after serving as the Chief of the Ambulance Service for the Griffin Spalding County Hospital for a brief time, he donned another. He became a peace officer. Perhaps no role was more challenging than this one, or more fitting for his unique wisdom, gifts, and faith.

He became a security officer specifically for death row inmates at the Georgia State Diagnostic Center in Jackson, Georgia. No doubt about it, his experiences as a security guard on death row had an impact on how he personally faced death, and how he would use the occasion of his own death to teach me and further prepare me for the work of ministry.

Mr. Charles did, and to this day does, hold a very special place with me. My dad, Tom Smith, knew that. And he knew, given my planned trip to Atlanta, there would be no way I would pass the Veterans Hospital and not stop to visit with Mr. Charles.

When I was told at the information desk that Mr. Charles was in a private critical care room within the cancer ward of the hospital, I instinctively knew that the prognosis would not be good. When upon entering the room, my eyes saw his terribly jaundiced condition and his weakened state, my thoughts were confirmed. My head knew and my heart hurt.

Mr. Charles was conscious, communicative, and thankfully not in any pain. He had several IV's, but he was quick to let me know that he was not knowingly taking any narcotics that would cloud either his ability to comprehend his surroundings or express his thoughts.

Also, in the room that day was Mrs. Eloise. It would be on subsequent visits that I would have the opportunity to visit and share with Danny, Maribeth and their younger brother, Tim.

After the hugs, upon that initial meeting, Mr. Charles and Mrs. Eloise shared the specifics of their situation.

Mr. Charles had terminal cancer. It had been discovered in his liver, hence the jaundice. The prognosis was that he might live yet a few weeks even if none of the efforts the doctors were making to slow the cancer's progression were effective. Of course, no one knew.

As he continued describing his illness, I noticed a stuffed animal tied atop one of his IV stands. I remember that smile and unmistakable chuckle as he explained after I curiously pointed my finger toward it that one of the grandchildren had brought the stuffed animal to him as a gift to remind him that they loved him.

He said as he smiled from ear to ear, "Logan, notice that of all things, it is a stuffed, crouched monkey. I told the child that, instead of sleeping with it, I was going to put it on top of the IV stand to remind us all to pray, because the monkey's really on my back."

That was just like Mr. Charles to see the humor in such a gift, and, given such circumstances, to use it to bless everyone. For nothing is more comforting than prayer in a time of stress when the monkey is on someone's back. Ask any Christian; they will all agree.

That is when Mr. Charles and Mrs. Eloise almost in concert said, "Logan, we know we have not seen each other for a long time, but we do not believe your coming today, of all days, is an accident. For we need your help."

"Of course," I said, "Name it!"

They explained, "We still attend the Rehoboth Baptist Church outside of Orchard Hill. Our minister is a good pastor and we love him. Recently, he was given the opportunity for an extended excursion, a sabbatical, to England. He just left this week. Of course, he said he did not want to leave us, and we knew he was sincere. But this opportunity for him is a once in a lifetime opportunity. We encouraged him to go.

"Given the prognosis of the physician, most likely he will not have returned before death comes. Will you stand in for him and help us through whatever time we have left together?" Then Mr. Charles added as Mrs. Eloise began to lightly sob, "Will you officiate at my funeral and help my family amid their grief?"

Without hesitation, I said, "Yes. I too grieve. But I will do whatever I can to minister to you all, amid whatever is ahead of us. I will be with you. And should your pastor return sooner than expected, I will support him as he ministers to us all."

Mr. Charles then reached for my hand which I extended. He cupped my hand in his, smiled as only he did, and said, "Thank you! But, son, I will tell you again, I do not believe you appeared today by chance. I am glad we are together again, and I know our Lord will see us all through."

Almost daily I began what for me was nothing less than extending a long-held love to a family that had faithfully loved me. It was amid the routine that I too began to become aware of the certain conviction that our Lord had indeed for this time brought us back together. But with that conviction there was the additional awareness of something more. Something yet to be revealed. Something yet to be learned.

That awareness was confirmed in less than two weeks of my initial hospital visit. Only Mr. Charles was in the room at the time I arrived. One thing caught my eye immediately. The monkey was no longer atop Mr. Charles' IV stand. In fact, I did not spot the monkey positioned anywhere.

Although when I first mentioned that fact my words were intended to be little more than a casual observance and informal greeting, immediately they became a springboard into the deepest level of communication within which I am convinced two people might ever engage.

With that unmistakable tone of voice that communicates nothing less than ultimate truth, complete honesty, uncompromised conviction, and what Jesus called, "The peace that surpasses all understanding." Mr. Charles said, "You are right son. The monkey is not on my IV stand anymore because it would be inappropriate for him to any longer be there. You see, the monkey is not on my back anymore."

"He's not?" I remarked.

"No," said he.

And I remember asking instinctively as I sought further to understand, only to become again the learner under the tutelage of Mr. Charles, "So, Mr. Charles, you have peace?" I asked.

He responded with what I perceived to be a divine grin and the wisdom of Solomon himself, "Yes, I have peace. Anyone living on death row had better have peace with God." And following a brief pause with a fixed, unbroken penetrating gaze he added, "And we all are, you know!"

Sensing he had yet more to share, I recall asking, "What has happened?"

He said, "I am not certain many people would believe me, but somehow I know you will accept that it happened just as I am describing it to you."

And he added, in words almost verbatim to those I had not

heard in over a decade and which had until that moment remained dormant, "I have had my visitation. I saw Him standing at the foot of my bed. The Lord said that I would be given a brief time to say goodbye, but it was time for me to come with Him. I don't know that I have ever experienced such love and affirmation. And there was one more thing. As the Lord was speaking to me, I was given a glimpse of heaven. Everything is so beautiful there. And I heard the heavenly choir singing. The music was indescribably beautiful. I suppose my only additional wish might have been for others to have seen Him and heard what I heard. But I realized quickly that only I could see and only I could hear. You tell everybody that everything is okay. Yes, I have peace and I have joy."

I continued to listen as Mr. Charles shared his thoughts about his recent experience of "visitation." Then we prayed together. Instinctively I knew that I was saying my final goodbye this side of heaven as I left the room.

It all occurred just as Mr. Charles had said. Less than forty-eight hours later the Lord stood again at the foot of his bed, and Mr. Charles, drawing his last earthly breath, went with Him.

At the moment of his death, an affirmation of the truth of all that Mr. Charles had shared with me occurred…a miracle that brought great comfort to others of the family, especially Mrs. Eloise as she had briefly left his room.

The miracle was that though standing in the hallway of the hospital on a lower floor, Mrs. Eloise knew that Mr. Charles had just left with Jesus because she heard. She heard as distinctly and definitively as one could ever hear the melody of that same heavenly music of which Mr. Charles had spoken. She described it this way, "Although there likely was not an instrument anywhere close to this hospital, it was the most beautiful organ music I had ever heard. Nothing on earth like it. I knew it was his way of saying it to me, 'Do not be afraid. It's all okay.'"

Perhaps one reason I remember so well the details of this event so many years ago is that I am reminded of them so often. You see, I was given two hundred dollars as a gift from Mr. Charles for officiating at his funeral. I did not desire any money, of course. But Mrs. Eloise insisted that it was Mr. Charles' wish that I have this gift.

Upon accepting the gift, it occurred to me how I might well perpetuate Mr. Charles' life and witness by investing the funds in my ministry. I had been saving to purchase a pulpit robe and vestments for use not only in formal worship, but at weddings and funerals.

In those days, the robe, which was considered expensive, was exactly one hundred ninety dollars, plus tax. I purchased the robe which served the intended purposes, also reminding me each time I wore it how Mr. Charles had experienced his divine visitation. I was pleased to know that the family seemed blessed by what I had done with the gift.

But note I said, "wore it." You see, approximately one year following Mr. Charles' death and the purchase of the robe, our local church facilities, inclusive of my office and study, were destroyed by fire.

Personal losses most significant to me included over two hundred volumes of my personal library, my young son's bronzed baby shoes, which served as bookends on my desk, and, yes, the robe.

The Ultimate Step

In the days following the fire, Mrs. Eloise, having learned of my losses through someone unknown to me, visited me at my house, which temporarily had also become the church office.

She asked if what she had been told was true concerning my personal losses in the church fire, expressing a definite interest in the robe. "Yes," I said. "It hurts me to know that the robe was destroyed."

It was then that she reached into her purse and retrieved her wallet. She dug deep into a hidden compartment within her wallet and withdrew two one- hundred-dollar bills. Pausing amid silent tears, she said, "Days before Charles's death he gave me these two bills. It was on the same occasion he gave me the two hundred dollars as a gift for you."

"He told me that he did not yet know why I would need them, but at the appropriate time I would know. But whatever I decided the occasion was, use the money in a way that would bring to me ultimate joy. I know in my heart now what the money is to do…take it, Logan. Let Charles and I replace the robe so that we both can continue to bear witness of our faith through you."

With trembling hands and tears in my own eyes, I accepted the money and bought a second pulpit robe, which I wear on appropriate occasions to this day. Every time I do so, I thank our Lord for the life and witness of brother Charles. That is one primary reason why these memories are so vivid almost forty years later.

Like my Uncle Bud, Mr. Charles had his visitation. Two very different men physically, academically, economically, and in almost every other way except two. One, I knew they loved me, and I loved them. And two, they were identical in their faith and experience of faith, especially amid the experience of death.

Both men testified that the Lord appeared to them and foretold exactly what was about to happen…and just as they both claimed, the events occurred.

I can still hear within my mind Mr. Charles asking as he said he did of others who could not, "Don't you see? Don't you hear?"

Did I at this point in my life reach all the conclusions I am yet to share about the Christian experience of death? One might think reading this that I should say "Yes." But, no, there were yet more occasions of dynamic revelation yet to come that would lead me to today's conviction.

What happened next?

Chapter 3

Nana

It was a lovely day. It was a Tuesday in 1991. All seemed right with the world especially in the deep south of Georgia. The sun was brightly shining. I could see as I drove south along the old coastal highway from Darien, Georgia, where I was now pastor of the First Baptist Church, to the city of Brunswick, Georgia, that the seas were calm.

And so was my spirit, except perhaps for that little voice within that kept tempting my resolve to stay on task and perform my ministerial duties of the afternoon which included visiting several patients at the Southeast Georgia Medical Center. That little voice kept saying, "With calm seas, clear skies, and a perfect mean low tide, everyone will understand if you take the afternoon off and go fishing. You know the sea trout and spot tail bass (some people call them "big reds") are just waiting to jump into your live well this afternoon and join you for supper."

But that other voice-- the responsibility voice-- was greater. So it was with a heart at peace, a smile on my face and a determined resolve to extend pastoral care to several of my church members in the hospital that I entered through the main entrance of the medical center, took the elevator, and began my round of visits on the first floor.

All was as expected until I stepped off the elevator to continue my visits to the patients on the third floor. Frankly, as others exiting the elevator with me, I was startled to hear the loud quarreling resounding from the room on the right almost a full hallway away.

One of the voices was familiar. It was she I was on my way to visit. I had been told that her mother-in-law, for whom she was the primary caregiver, had been hospitalized due to a severe illness, the specifics of which were not known to me. I had also been told that Beth, the daughter-in-law, was sitting virtually around the clock assisting in every possible way.

I did not know Beth's mother-in-law. She was not a member of my congregation. It had long been my conviction that caregivers often needed as much support and pastoral care as the patients themselves. That is why I had decided before arriving at the hospital that I would make this visit to affirm and pray with both Beth and her mother-in-law, whom I learned was affectionately called, "Nana."

Beth was an industrious young woman in her mid-thirties. Although her profession was that of a successful elementary school administrator, like many admirable women, her vocation was much broader based. Other areas of her vocation included the roles of wife, mother, homemaker, and extended family nurturer, as well as caregiver.

Prior to this occasion, I do not recall having heard Beth raise her voice at anyone. Rather, Beth had always seemed in every situation to be both in control and tempered in her response. If anything, she had always seemed to be very measured, if not slightly reserved, in publicly addressing any issue.

That is why upon immediately hearing her frustrated and angry voice echoing down the hospital corridor as I was exiting the elevator, it is an understatement to say that I experienced a complete surprise and a degree of shock. I noticed two nurses bounding toward the room as did I undoubtedly in hopes of calming the situation which certainly was becoming more and more disturbing and disruptive to other visitors, patients, and caregivers on the floor.

One of the nurses whom I had gotten to know while serving as a voluntary chaplain for this hospital reached to alert the other nurse of my presence, looked toward me and said, "There is Dr. Smith. I am certain he can help."

"I will," I said without missing a step. All three of us traversed the hall in record time. I entered the patient's room through the open door to see Beth with her hands high in the air screaming, "Please, please, stop yelling, lie down and try to go to sleep."

Also, there was distraught "Nana" who had the typical appearance of a Norman Rockwell grandmother. She was in her eighth decade. Her face bore the deep furrows of years of hard work and coping with challenges neither my nor Beth's generation had ever faced. Her hair was very thin, but distinctly white with a tinge of gray. Yet it was obvious her hair style and its care were important to her. In the tradition of the old south, it was colored and styled to communicate that she was a lady in every sense of the word. And make no mistake about it, she was.

Yet here she was in response to Beth's desperation likewise flailing the air with her erratic arm movements and screaming,

"Quit telling me what to do and listen. You are always telling me what to do and it is you, not me, who is going to shut-up and listen!"

It was a dramatic scene thick with the deepest of emotions no Hollywood screen writer could ever have adequately scripted or actors fully portrayed.

But moments after I entered room, everything, and I stress "everything," suddenly changed. Both women suddenly quit screaming and Nana, again whom I had never met, did a most unusual thing.

Nana, now in total control of her behavior, turned her attention away from Beth, stared at me with a fixed gaze as if from a world beyond, pointed the index finger of her right hand at me while extending her arm fully, and said in a voice with gravity and an unmistakable existential emphasis, "You know! You know! You know!"

Then, after a pause and a few moments of stunned recognition on the part of Beth and the nurses who remained motionless and quiet, instinctively realizing that something beyond the realm of normalcy was taking place, Nana added, "Ask him. He knows! He knows!"

Just as suddenly, I knew she was right. I did know. Call it what you will: intuition, spiritual inspiration, or epiphany, but I did instantaneously know. Looking back at her, directly into her eyes, and perhaps through them down the corridors of her heart to the very depths of her soul, I knew. I knew that this elder woman whom heretofore I had never met perceived that she was dying. I knew that she was desperately trying to communicate something before the imminent moment of her death occurred.

I said to her words that did bring an instantaneous calm to the chaotic moment. I said, "Yes, I do know." Then, still directly staring into my eyes, dropping her voice from the epitome of rage to normalcy, she said, "Yes. You do."

I asked, "Would you allow me to step outside into the hallway with Beth for a moment, so that as the nurses assist you, I might explain everything to her?" As I hopefully anticipated she said, "Please."

Somewhat stunned by what she had just witnessed and heard, Beth without commenting stepped outside into the hallway as the nurses attended to Nana, helping her to comfortably settle again back into her bed. Undoubtedly, they double-checked the IV attachment and the monitor displays. And rather than chide her, they quizzed her on her needs and wishes. Then they returned to their other duties with a smile and a "thank you" as they stepped around Beth and me in the hallway.

Beth turned to me with a disturbed, but sincere question, "Preacher, what in the world is going on? I do not understand Nana. We have never argued this way before. Nana has never refused to at least consider what I have to say. It is almost like she has lost her mind. She has not eaten, nor has she slept, in nearly two days although the whole family keeps telling her that she needs to do so."

Seeking to reaffirm, I said kindly, "Beth, do not panic. Just take a deep breath and try to be calm for a moment. I understand that you love Nana. And because of your love for her, you are frustrated, confused and afraid. But trust me."

Then as I had suggested, Beth took several deep breaths. As she did, her trembling hands began to calm. As she regained her composure, she said, "Ask him. He knows. What do you know?"

I responded honestly and directly, "Nana believes that she is going to die. She believes her death is imminent. I do not know if what she believes is true. I only know that she believes that it is so. I also know that there is something that she is desperately trying to communicate before her moment of death comes, something that is most important to her and she believes is vital to you and the rest of the family."

"But…" said Beth, "Nobody has said anything about her dying. The doctors have told us that her illness is serious, but everybody expects her with the treatment she is receiving to recover. I believe if she will just start eating, getting some rest, and sleeping, she will start feeling better and fully recover."

"I understand," I said, "You may be exactly right in your assessment. But whatever the truth about her condition may be, she believes she is about to die. My suggestion is simply this: Let the two of us go back into the room. You introduce me formally to Nana. Then you say to her, 'Nana, I will listen, and I promise not to interrupt. Tell me whatever it is that you have been trying to communicate to me. I will do my best to comply with whatever requests you have.'" Following a brief pause I asked, "Beth, will you do this promising not to verbally discount or call into question anything Nana says?"

Beth thought for a moment and responded, "I will try. But it will not be easy."

"You are right," I said, "Such occasions are never easy, but I have never known them to be unimportant or unmeaningful. Again, just listen, if for no other reason, because at this moment this is what Nana needs. It might be the best medicine you could ever give to her."

Most appropriately, as her minister, I returned the very light embrace which with a tear she extended to me. We then reentered Nana's room. Beth walked up to her bedside, laid her hand upon Nana's hand, and spoke directly from her heart.

She said, "Nana, I am sorry. I am sorry that I kept arguing with you instead of listening to you. Pastor Logan has explained everything to me. Please share with me again what it is you have been trying to tell me."

Nana placed her other hand on top of Beth's hand before Beth ever finished her statement. As Beth paused, Nana said, "I love you, too, so very much."

Nana continued, "That is why it is not without sadness I have to let you know that I am dying. I am going to greatly miss you and the whole family until the day when I pray, we will all be together again."

"You must tell all the family that what means the most to me now is that they all believe in and love Jesus as I do as both their Savior and Lord. For that alone assures me of a heavenly family reunion. I want you to give to them some personal messages that now I know I will not have the time or occasion to share myself.

"Will you get a pen and paper and write the messages down as I share them with you so that you can more easily, and without worrying about remembering everything, share the messages personally with each family member?"

Thankfully, a pen and writing pad were nearby. Of course, Beth agreed. Nana added, "Pastor, if you have the time, will you stay until we are finished writing the messages. I will then have one final request to make of you."

I said, "Certainly!" thinking that surely at that point she would most likely ask that I say a prayer for her, Beth, and the family. Almost without exception, that is the last request made of any minister upon a hospital visit.

Then Nana proceeded. She began with a note to her older son followed by another to her younger daughter. She then had words of comfort and counsel to each of her grandchildren. She had instructions to certain extended family members and a few friends. She even had a sentence or two for the funeral director, whom she had long ago prepaid for all her burial expenses.

The dialogue between Nana and Beth, along with the recording of the information, took somewhere around forty-five minutes to an hour. Each message from Nana to her family was well-thought-through and deeply heart felt. I felt sincerely complimented that Nana had not asked me, as a stranger, to leave the room. There was a depth of privilege and communication to it all that I can only describe as intimate and holy.

Finally, Nana said to Beth, who had kept her word by not second guessing anything that Nana had said, "That is it, darling. And thank you, thank you for being the one perfect wife to my son and daughter to me."

Their embrace was a testimony to the depth of love only two such women could ever know. It was something, I think, akin to Ruth and Naomi of the Old Testament writings.

Nana turned to me and asked, "Pastor, would you come over to the side of my bed?" But instead of asking me to pray, she said, "Would you hold my hand as I leave?"

Then she added, "And, Beth, will you hold my other hand. That is how I want to go." Beth softly said, "Go?"

"Yes," said Nana. "I am going to heaven now. It's okay. It is time and I am ready. I want to go. I will miss you, but I will see you."

Turning to me still again, she said, "Thank you pastor, for seeing me over."

Nana closed her eyes. She took a deep breath. For the first time in two days she lay comfortably as one initiating a long night's rest. Beth looked at me as if to ask, "What now?" I simply placed a finger upon my lips to indicate continued silence.

In about a minute or so, I expected Nana not necessarily to die, but to fall asleep. But instead, shortly after having closed her eyes while holding our hands, I noticed three surprising things.

First, the grip of Nana's hand tightened upon mine. It was not as one might expect when experiencing pain or distress, but rather a gentle tightening as if something very dynamic and pleasurable was happening, or about to happen.

Second, I noticed tears. I noticed a tear from each of Nana's eyes slowly trickling down from the corner of her eye to beneath her fading hairline.

A few seconds later, I noticed Nana's third reaction. Her wrinkled chin began to quiver. That is when I knew. Nana was not going to sleep, rather Nana was weeping.

Knowing how confident and courageous she had been only moments ago, I asked sympathetically, "Nana, why do you weep?"

She said, "It is so beautiful. So very, very beautiful."

"What are you seeing Nana? What is so beautiful?" I asked.

"Heaven," she said. "I can see heaven. The colors are so vivid, so alive. All the colors are there. The city itself is golden. It really is! And everything is so bright!... And the flowers! Their colors and fragrances are magnificent. I want to go there. I never want to leave there.

"And there is Jesus. He is speaking to me. Yes! He is speaking to me. And He is beautiful, too. His eyes are full of compassion. His voice is so tender and so full of love. He is telling me that it is all true, what I have believed all these years. He loves me. I feel it and I know it. Never have I felt as loved as I do now. No one has or could possibly ever love me more.

"I want to be with Him in this wonderful place. I know He wants me there, too. I want to go. I want to go now."

Nana paused as the tears began to flow more freely. I felt compelled to ask, "Nana, seeing that heaven is so beautiful, seeing that Jesus is so glorious, and knowing that He loves you so, why do you weep?"

Nana, squeezing my hand with a more forceful grip, opened her eyes, and through her tears in a clear, distinctive voice said, "Because He says that I cannot come, at least not yet. I want to go and be with Him now."

She closed her eyes again as if merely redirecting her gaze. Her words were, "Please let me come. Please let me come now. Please do not make me wait." Then her tears progressed into sobs.

After a brief period of sobbing, a time during which Beth nor I dared to speak, Nana again opened her eyes and said, "He doesn't tell me why I cannot come now although I wish I knew. He just tells me that I must wait. He tells me that I must wait three days …. three days … then I can come to be with Him. But I do not want to wait even three days."

The Ultimate Step

Then she looked still again directly into my eyes and asked, "Why, why does Jesus say that I have to wait three days?"

I replied, "Sister, I do not know. I have no idea why our Lord is telling you that you must wait three days before going to Heaven to be with Him. I can only think that possibly He needs you to stay those three days that He might yet somehow speak and teach through you. Possibly He needs your waiting to afford a member of your family or someone else the opportunity to learn about Him, life, death, and heaven. I do not know. But with you I will simply trust Him to keep His word and to continue loving and holding on to you and me."

Wiping away the tears that continued to flow, Nana said, "If that is what He wants, what He needs, so be it. But I do want to go to be with Him. Having seen how lovely He is, experienced how beautiful heaven is, and felt how indescribably wonderful is His love for me, I want to go now!"

I said to Nana, as Beth also had begun to weep, "Well, in the meantime, do you think that you might try to simply rest as you think about what you have seen and heard?" To which she responded, "I am so very, very tired now. I think I shall."

For the first time in two days Nana slept. Beth and I left the room after Nana fell asleep. In the hospital corridor we prayed. I left the hospital pondering what I had seen and heard.

Beth would phone me later in the evening that same day. She shared how Nana had slept peaceably for several hours. Upon awaking, Nana had commented that she was hungry. For the first time in nearly three days she enjoyed a meal.

Other than Beth's husband, no other family member had to my knowledge come to the hospital. So only Beth and Phillip were with her still later that evening when it happened. A nurse came into the room to check Nana's vital signs only to discover that she could not awaken her.

Although her vital signs were stable, according to the physician, Nana had inexplicably fallen into a coma. She was taken from her private room to the hospital's intensive care unit on a lower floor. There, the larger family eventually gathered. They coordinated an around the clock vigil, anticipating that when Nana awoke, a member of the family would be with her.

That vigil was maintained faithfully. And I was there. I was there three days to the hour when Nana's prophetic vision came true. Three days to the very hour, and only our Lord knows if to the very minute, the doctor with an accompanying nurse asked us all to come back from the waiting area to Nana's small room within the intensive care unit where he informed us that Nana had unexpectedly passed away.

We all were afforded the opportunity to say goodbye, but not forever; rather only for a while, a fact of which I reminded us all as the family wept and many of them for a final time kissed her brow. But I confess that, even then, I wondered, "What did these three days of waiting accomplish? Who was it that Nana remained to teach?"

Although I could not begin to answer those questions, and I still cannot, I knew this much. I could not deny the truth of Nana's own words. She was exactly right about three days, which validates her other claims, as far as I am concerned. She had been given a vision. She had experienced her own visitation. She had seen a glimpse of heaven. She had seen the Lord.

She faced the moment of her death confidently, courageously, even eagerly, as did Uncle Bud and Mr. Charles. And like Uncle Bud and Mr. Charles, she did not face death alone.

That is the primary thought and revelation that I perceived and documented on the day of Nana's death. But even as I have been writing these words, another thought has come to mind.

The thought is this, and in no way do I seek to be presumptuous: Am I the person who needed Nana to delay for three days entering heaven? Could I be the person who needed her witness for the very purpose of the writing of this book? Or could that person be you, as you read her story? Could her lessons about life, death, love and the Lord Jesus be for you for the purpose of comforting you in light of a loved one's death, or for the purpose of encouraging and strengthening you in light of the inevitability of your own death?

I have an idea that the correct answer to these questions is, to varying degrees, "All of the above."

I know this much. Decades later, I can still within the sound chambers of my mind hear Nana saying, "Heaven is so beautiful. Jesus is so loving. I want to go and be with Him now!"

Chapter 4

Sis

The year 1991 would witness still another dynamic and unusual revelation of a Christian's encounter with death. Her name was Ann. However, no one except her family, intimate friends and the DMV knew her by that name. She seemed known to one and all as simply "Sis."

I understand that the name "Sis" had been perpetuated throughout her life by her elder sister, Elaine, who simply had referred to Ann as "Sis" since she was first able to speak as a child. Knowing how well "Sis" was known by that name, I can only wonder if her deceased husband, who I never had the privilege of meeting, had called her by that name.

Nevertheless, from the day I first met her as her new pastor in the mid 1980's, "Sis" she was.

Sis and her elder sister were both in their late seventies, widowed, and living together just up the street from the pastorium. As many such female "elder women who stylishly color coordinate their tennis shoes," and I use that metaphor strictly as a compliment, they seemed to both have been ladies of some means although they lived modestly.

Their pride and joy? Their children and grandchildren, of course. In 1991, Sis was eagerly anticipating the birth of another grandchild, while likewise anticipating the wedding of still another.

And how would I describe "Sis?" Well, she was a southern lady, to be certain, but she was no passive "china doll." She had experienced many good times. She had endured many difficult times. As a result, she was one of the toughest but most tender of women I ever met.

The attributes of toughness and tenderness were hers both physically and spiritually. For instance, I recall one so-called "minor" surgical procedure that was to have kept her bed ridden for at least a month, only to see her once home from the hospital just a few days after surgery, outside in her garden tending to her flowers. "Can't let anything keep you down," she repeatedly said. "You have to keep moving."

And should you ever had said, "But you must take care of yourself," I know exactly what she repeatedly would have said in response: "That is what I am doing. Two things I never, never do. I do not worry about anything. That is a waste of energy and time. I do not sit around. That will destroy anybody."

So, to say that "Sis" was simply industrious, tough, and determined is, in my opinion, all understatements. She was a lady who not only set goals but worked arduously to achieve them. She saw a task that needed doing, and with zeal she did it. And grace be to anyone or anything who attempted to deter her from accomplishing whatever she set out to do and believed was right.

But do not allow me to distort her image. While being so "tough," as I said, she was also "tender." She was one of the sweetest and kindest ladies I have ever had the privilege of knowing.

Her kindness was reflected in both her voice and her actions. She had those mothering attributes that transcended her smile, her polite handshake, her light embrace. Greater still, she never hesitated to extend those attributes to others in need of them.

Yes, that was "Sis" … and maybe that is why others preferred to call her "Sis" rather than Ann.

And on Sundays? Except for rare exceptions, look from the pulpit to the fifth row to the right near the stain-glassed windows, and there you would see her actively participating in the worship hour. And at the conclusion of the service never did she leave the sanctuary without a kind word and the shaking of the pastor's hand with a promise the pastor instinctively knew was sincere: "I will be praying for you Pastor." She was the senior adult model every Pastor wishes others would emulate.

I never knew her to be aggressive in the sharing of her faith, but she was not shy about it either. I can only imagine what she might have said to someone who claimed to be "offended" by the mention of Christ or His witness. She was a Christian. And she offered not the slightest apology for her faith.

I still recall the occasion when Sis with her strong sense of conviction served the church in a most unique way. I do not recall the month. I only remember that it was in the Spring of the year amid what was traditionally, within the church, called "revival time."

One of the fine senior adult men of our congregation rushed into my office one morning apparently still in shock in response to what he had just experienced. It happened as he was getting his morning mail from the city post office, as was his daily custom.

Describing the event to me, he said, "As I was looking over the envelopes I had received, a friend of mine from nearby Eulonia walked in, and we began to chat.

"As we were talking, it occurred to me that I had in the pocket of my coat one of our revival flyers. It just seemed like the opportune moment for me to invite him to come and worship with us. I took the revival flyer out of my pocket, extended it to him, and urged him to come and bring his whole family to the revival services.

"But hardly had I worded the invitation when the local police chief, who I was not even aware was in the post office, much less listening to our conversation, tapped me on my shoulder. He snatched the revival flyer out of my hand. He told me that I was breaking the law by soliciting at the post office without a license. He gave me this ticket, telling me that he would look forward to my appearing in court.

"Pastor, I did not know that it was illegal to invite someone to attend church anywhere. What do I do?"

I remember telling him, "You do not do anything. Do not worry. Just go home and let me see what I can do to help you. I will call you later."

He was still shaken when he left my office. I immediately asked my secretary to reach the Mayor of the city on the telephone. We both knew that he would likely be in his office at the local supermarket that he owned and managed.

The mayor was a Presbyterian churchman, a good man, and a friend. I knew, however, that this did not mean that my intervention in this matter would be welcomed. For as sincere as his faith was, and I do not question it, he was fiercely guarded when it came to city politics, employees, and related matters. He was particularly sensitive when it came to "legal" matters.

It was only a matter of minutes before I had the opportunity to say to him, "Mr. Mayor, we have to talk. I have a matter of great legal concern that I wish to discuss with you concerning the actions of your chief of police toward one of the elderly men in my congregation. You and I both know that the chief is no friend of the church, but this time he has gone too far."

I do not know if it was the demeanor in my voice or just the mere mention of the word "legal" that prompted it. But the mayor responded, "No. Do not come to my office; I will come to your office."

Less than a half hour later, the mayor arrived at my office with his comrade in arms, the head of the city council, who also worked at his supermarket. I could sense immediately that they were not glad that I had called. Also, they had already talked to the police chief, and from their opening remarks, were not only prepared to defend the police chief, but to put me back in my place.

After they had finished their rebuttal to my inquiry, I remember saying, "Mr. Mayor, Mr. Councilman, you have been wanting to put our small hamlet on the map. This just might do it. For if you are asserting that it is illegal to publicly invite someone to attend church, I will have to get more involved, and I assure you we will get plenty of statewide, if not national attention.

"Before the day is out, we will make the press. I will alert the Southern Baptist Convention and engage their legal department. I will contact the Georgia Baptist Convention within which I serve and engage both their legal teams and their state-wide press, 'The Christian Index.' I will place a call to my dear friend, our state senator, and get the capitol involved. I will contact my friend, the news anchor for the television station in Savannah, and give him the exclusive story. If it is now publicly illegal to invite individuals to attend church in our city, I will indeed help you to put it on the map."

Then I know I must have grinned as a greater threat came to mind. I said, "But if I were you, I would not worry about any of these things. What I would worry about are all the little old marvelous ladies in my congregation and yours who will not appreciate such a law. And when I tell 'Sis,' and you know Sis, she can help me immediately get the word out to all the people in town, and you will probably have at one time more visitors to your supermarket than you have had in a long time."

I noticed his eyes light up when I mentioned Sis. He also knew her courage and zeal as well as her influence upon others. The mayor simply said, "We will be back in touch."

And they were. Within an hour there was another meeting in my office. This time the mayor, the councilman, the police chief, and my elder church member were all present. To sum it up: the police chief apologized to the elderly church member. The ticket was destroyed. Promises were made that no such actions would be repeated in the future. Everybody shook hands upon leaving, even although those handshakes probably meant little more than, "We are glad nobody got shot today."

I cannot help but to this day think that maybe more people would be spared unnecessary suffering if there were more leaders like Sis around. Sis was a Christian and unashamedly so. She was courageous as well as straightforward in her faith. And in a marvelous way, she made certain you knew it. For at the root of it all, she wanted you to be a person of faith, too. That is why the people who knew her did not fear her as much as they respected her. Our small hamlet was a better place because Sis was in it.

But that same year, 1991, I would witness a day of unexpected, drastic changes for Sis. As sudden as the cold front that was ushered in by the northeaster that day in our small coastal town came the onset of the deterioration of Sis's health.

She was rushed twelve miles away to the nearest hospital after having collapsed at the local post office within walking distance of her home. Numerous "mini-strokes" were the initial diagnosis, although no drastic extensions of paralyses manifested themselves.

And while some symptoms commonly associated with a stroke did arise, other problems rapidly seemed to multiply as various systems within her body were affected. Within just a couple of days, Sis deteriorated from her robust, active self to being confined to a critical care unit where she was literally fighting for her life.

Sis was granted a respite. Hardly surprising to the attending physicians who knew of Sis's strong will and constitution, she did begin after a few days of critical care to show signs of possible recovery. It was a day of celebration for Sis and the family when she was moved to a private room within the hospital.

The celebration was further enhanced when, after a week or so, the doctor informed the family that Sis could leave the hospital. However, Sis must not yet return home. He preferred that she be admitted to a rehabilitation unit located at a nursing care facility nearby on St. Simons Island.

Immediately, a large private room, normally designed for two patients rather than one, was secured for her. Shortly thereafter, she was relocated. All seemed to suggest that her health would continue to improve.

But it was not to be. As I returned home around dusk of that memorable day, having been visiting another church member, my wife informed me that family members were trying to reach me about another change in Sis's health condition.

I returned a phone call to one of the children, who explained that Sis had experienced another stroke episode that had left her in a coma. Further, Sis had been taken to the hospital, but returned to the nursing care facility where critical care was available. The doctors simply said, "We are doing for her all we know to do. We are keeping her comfortable. We believe the nursing care facility will afford to you, the family, and her the more ideal opportunity for mutual care, given that we are simply waiting to see how she will yet respond."

The family was very direct in their expressed understanding of what they believed the doctors were saying. They said, "We believe that the doctors are telling us that Sis is not only in a coma, but she is dying. We knew you would want to know."

After hanging up the telephone, I told my wife, "I have to go and check on Sis." To this day I do not know what compelled me to do it, because I cannot remember another such occasion when I did so. But I turned to my young teenage son standing nearby and asked, "Sis is very, very ill, and I must go to the nursing home on St. Simons Island to check on her, would you like to go with me?"

To my surprise, he said, "Dad, it would mean a lot to me if I could go with you." I am gratified to this day that my son, now in his forties, recalls the events just as I am describing them to you.

The Ultimate Step

We drove directly to the nursing care facility. Upon entering Sis's room, I was somewhat surprised, although not intending to be critical of anyone present, at what I observed. Just inside the door to the left was a small sitting area where several of the family members were gathered.

I understood that they were processing their emotions as families who are close and strong in their faith sometimes do. They were not quiet and tearful, rather they were laughing and loud, almost as if they were at a jovial dinner party. Their attention was focused on each other, rather than on Sis, who lay upon a single bed positioned in a corner completely across the room. I was curious at the lack of furniture and empty space between the two.

They acknowledged our arrival with a warm and polite greeting, whereupon I said, "We would like to have a brief visit and prayer with Sis."

One of the daughters responded, revealing that she did not understand the dynamics of a "coma" or Sis's condition, "Go ahead, preacher. But she will never know that you have been here. She is in a coma, so she cannot see or hear anything. We are all just waiting."

I remember thinking, "How do you know she cannot hear anything? How do you know she is not aware of her surroundings? That is why physicians often encourage visitors of comatose patients to speak to them and read aloud to them. More than a few patients have 'awakened' only to describe actual events and conversations that have taken place in their room while others thought they were totally unconscious." Nevertheless, I responded only with a smile: "I understand what you are saying. I would still like to have a few moments with her."

Of course, there was no objection. The family was most polite and gracious. While my son and I walked across the room to Sis, the family returned to their jovial conversation.

As I looked down at Sis, who appeared to be sleeping comfortably, it happened. It was another of those unusual moments I can only use the word "epiphany" to describe. I knew immediately what the others in the room would describe as "impossible," but what was nevertheless true.

I placed my hand upon Sis's and said while looking directly into her face, "Sis, they do not have any idea, do they? They do not understand, do they?"

She silenced the cacophony of sound in the room by opening her eyes and responding, "Not a darn thing, preacher, not a darn thing."

The thought did occur to me that it was as if I was looking into Nana's face all over again. So, I asked, "Sis, tell me where you were. Tell me what you are experiencing."

Sis said, "Preacher, I am caught between two worlds…this world and heaven. I do want to go to heaven, but I must be honest. I do want to meet my new grandchild and attend my granddaughter's wedding before I go. At this moment I am terribly torn."

I remember saying, "That is the most difficult thing about death, isn't it?" And she said, "It certainly is. It is not the dying, preacher; anybody can die, and everyone will. It is not the dying. It is the leaving! If you could take all your loved ones with you, who would not want to immediately go? We all would. But the thought of leaving, being separated from the people I love even for a while, is painful to me."

Then following a moment of silence, she added, "The Lord does not seem at all upset with me that I feel this way. He understands. He knows I love Him, too. He knows I want to be with Him. And I know He loves me."

I asked, "How do you know Sis?"

Said she amid tears I knew I had seen before, "Because He told me so."

"He told you?" I commented.

"Yes. He has already been to see me. He came to see me after I was brought back to the hospital. He told me that I would be coming to heaven very soon. He told me that my place in heaven was ready for me. And when I shared with Him what I shared with you, He just smiled. And I did so want to go with Him… I am just torn."

I said, "Sis, as much as it is possible for me, I understand. I have an idea that if in any way heaven would be compromised for you if you could not see that grandchild or celebrate the marriage of the other grandchild, Jesus will make a way for that compromise not to be so. Possibly, if it means all that heaven can be for you, Jesus will provide a way for you to do both…to go be with Him and still celebrate the wedding and the birth."

Said she, "I believe that too. And I know He is coming back to get me soon because He told me He was. I think I will tell Him that I will leave all my concerns to Him and go with Him. Let them all know, preacher, especially my daughter and my granddaughter, that I will be watching them. Tell them I am with Jesus, and everything is okay."

She then took a deep breath. I said a prayer. Her last words to me were, "Thank you, pastor, I think I will rest now."

Having said goodbye to Sis and the other members of the family, my son and I were walking across the parking lot when my son asked, "Do you really think that Jesus actually came to see her and spoke with her as she said?"

"Yes son, I do." I replied, "You see, she is not the first person to describe such a visitation. I have had other people over the years share similar experiences. Everything these people have described to me has been consistent, and the time frames they described to me have all proven to be true. So, again, yes, I do believe. If Jesus told her that He will be back for her soon, He will be."

My son said as we got into the car and buckled up our seatbelts, "Dad, until tonight, I do not think I have ever fully understood what as a minister besides preach you really do. But now I do. And I am glad."

At the conclusion of the thirty-minute drive home, my son and I noticed almost simultaneously that his mother, Carol, was standing on the front porch.

As we approached, she said, "I have been waiting for you. Logan, you need to go back to the nursing home." Then she explained, "The family needs you and called requesting that you come. Sis has died. They said that you had hardly left the room when she took one final deep breath and went to be with the Lord as she had told you she would. They tried to catch you before you got away. They made it to the parking area just as you turned onto the street. But you did not hear them yelling for you to come back or see them waving." Noticing that I checked the time by glancing at my watch, she added, "They said they knew it would take nearly an hour for you to both arrive at home and return to the island, but they will wait. They really want to talk."

I returned to the island and met with the family. I cannot explain the delay, but Sis's body was only then being placed in the hearse from the local funeral home.

The family's questions were the same questions asked by my son. "Do you believe she really saw Jesus as she said? Do you believe she will actually be watching from heaven to witness both the birth and the wedding she so desperately wanted to see?" And then they asked, "How did you know, having taken only one look at her lying there, that she was not in a coma?"

My answers to all their questions can be summed up this way. "I do not have an explanation as to how I knew when I looked at her that Sis was not in a coma. My only certainty is that by the inspiration of the Holy Spirit alone I just at that moment knew. And yes, I take Sis at her word that Jesus had visited with her and was coming again soon to take her to heaven. After all, the evidence is that she was exactly right. Her last words to me are the ones she wanted me to stress with you. 'Tell them that I am with Jesus and that everything is okay.'"

The family and I continued to talk for some time. We then prayed together and returned to our respective homes.

Why do I share Sis's story when it seems to only replicate the previous ones I have documented in this book? Essentially, because Sis worded that additional dimension, that one insight into the death experience I had never heard more beautifully or, I believe, accurately, stated.

She said it so beautifully and succinctly, and now, thirty years later, nearing my seventh decade and being three years what they call a "cancer survivor," I absolutely agree:" It is not the dying, or the changing of worlds, that is our source of such great grief or loss when death comes, it is the leaving." It is the simple reality of being separated from those we so deeply love, even more so than any fear or anxiety regarding the unknown.

That fact alone makes "the visitation" of Jesus infinitely more precious. For that separation of love can be made bearable, even for a while, by the presence of another who loves.

All the stories I have related thus far share that common fact. Uncle Bud, Mr. Charles, Nana and Sis each spoke of their visitation of Jesus's coming with love.

Separated from loved ones in death? Yes! But from love altogether? For the Christian? Absolutely not! We are never separated from the love of Jesus, who loves us unconditionally, although we are separated from others we love only for a while.

Is there yet another story that I believe needs to be told that would add further insight into our understanding of a Christian's death? I think so.

But before I share the next occasion of great insight for me, may I make one suggestion? Pause your reading and by whatever means necessary and available, go tell your loved ones how much you sincerely love them. Do not assume they know, even if they do. Tell them. Say it. Kiss them. Hug them.

For the day is coming, believe me, believe Sis, when your greatest desire regarding such an occasion will be, "Just One More Time."

Chapter 5

Old Joe

The story of Old Joe is somewhat unique in comparison to the others I cite in this collection as we discuss the death experience of a Christian.

His story also takes place in the small coastal community of Darien of South Georgia. Old Joe was not a member of my congregation, nor to my knowledge did he ever formally join any church.

My limited relationship with Old Joe evolved simply because he was married to Leah. Leah, like Old Joe, was amid her sixties when I became her pastor. She was another of those marvelous senior adults from whom the pastor draws strength. She was kind, sweet, certain of her faith, committed to Jesus Christ her Lord, and supportive in her prayers, as well as through her actions.

Within the church, Leah served faithfully. If a person was ill, she was there offering her assistance. If a person as a caregiver was stretched in their ability to cope, she was there to offer relief, support, and a respite. If a person was bereaved, she was there with a delectable dish in hand, followed by others she recruited to relieve any distress and perform daily essential tasks.

And Leah was like Martha of the New Testament in still another way. She understood what ladies of the south call "social graces." Although I never dined in her home, I would imagine that the salad fork was never missing nor out of place.

But she was not conspicuous or "showy" with her social graces. She was most often quiet and reserved, but not shy. She was genuinely modest both in her demeanor as well as in her dress and lifestyle.

She sang in the church choir faithfully in the soprano section every Sunday. I never heard her sing a solo, but given the enthusiasm she expressed as she sang, no doubt her voice was integral to the choir's beautiful music that enhanced our worship each Sunday.

And there was one other most pronounced characteristic of Leah that no one who met her failed to notice. Leah walked with a severe limp that made every step for her a challenge. Her disability was demonstrably significant because it enhanced and validified her servant's heart and sincere faith. I have witnessed others bewail their limitations and inabilities to live, love and serve that to no degree compared to Leah's challenge just to take another step.

But Leah persisted, something she had determined and succeeded in doing since she was a child. You see, Leah was not born with this disability. And it was not the result of some untimely accident. Rather, sometime around her tenth birthday, she, along with many other children at the time, contracted polio.

And while some individuals who suffered from that horrible disease became embittered, she did not. All I ever heard her express was gratitude. Whereas massive iron lungs, lingering disabilities, and early death became the fate of so many, she repeatedly said, "I may limp, but I was blessed with life."

Possibly that explains Leah's faith and servant's heart. For this, I believe, is a biblical truth, one I have seen manifested in others throughout the years: People who are grateful for having received grace, become increasingly grateful and graceful people who give grace out of their gratitude to others who will receive it.

Leah had among several stack poles of priorities in her life one she was always open and eager to discuss. She had one child, a son, whom she, in no unhealthy way, simply adored. She and this son had a mutually tight bond. Although at the time Leah and I met, the son had married and out of vocational necessity moved to another town, they still communicated with each other every day.

But most significantly, Leah drew strength from him to face every new day-- no doubt, the same way she had since the day of his birth. I believe this to be true because Leah had--and I mean no unethical disrespect toward anyone involved--another challenge to face in order to live life as Jesus described it, "abundantly"(see John 10:10 KJV).

I refer to Old Joe. Leah and Old Joe met as young teenagers. Leah was still a teenager when she married Old Joe, who was only twenty years of age. Not long after their marriage, Old Joe, and I am not certain whether he was drafted or volunteered, entered the military. He discovered quickly that he was most aptly suited for military service. As a result, he intended to continue his military career until the appropriate time for his retirement.

However, it was not to be. Old Joe eventually would find himself in the arena of war. The conflict would not leave him unscathed. From a bullet wound and shrapnel wounds to the legs and arms, Old Joe would recover. But from the emotional wounds he suffered not only as a result of his own physical injuries, but from his eyes having seen on the battlefield things a person should never have to see, his ears having heard things a person should never have to hear, and his "existential heart" having to cope with the death of friends and all the questions only a survivor of such a moment asks, Old Joe would remain to his dying day, to a degree, a casualty of war.

With these injuries, his military career did not last as he had hoped. And, regrettably, no other career ever adequately filled the void as Old Joe worked at one profession a few years before transitioning to another. At the time I first met Old Joe, he was semi-retired, occasionally working either as a deck hand on a local shrimp boat or a carpenter's helper on a small construction job. As one might imagine, whatever Old Joe did, he seemed to achieve his best when left largely to work alone, utilizing his hands.

So the Old Joe that eventually went off to war was not entirely the same Old Joe that came home from war. But Leah loved him just the same and remained faithful to Old Joe and their marriage vows until the day of her death.

I have no doubt that Old Joe loved her and their son, although until the final conversation Old Joe and I ever had, I never saw or heard from him the slightest kind gesture or word that I would call "demonstrative" toward either of them. In fact, I rarely saw Old Joe at all. For when I did try to visit and initiate a relationship with him, I was consistently met with little more than contempt usually expressed as, "What are you doing here? I have told you before that I have no use for the church, preachers, or that Christianity stuff."

Yet, I would occasionally try again, knowing that not a day passed that Leah was not praying for Old Joe to be healed completely, and foremost for him to commit his life to Jesus Christ as his Lord and Savior. Of course, Old Joe knew that Leah was praying, too. He himself would sometimes allude to that fact commenting, "I wish Leah would get off my back about this Jesus thing. But I suppose she never will."

To describe Old Joe as I would more than a few other such traumatized individuals I have known over my almost three score and ten years: he was loved yet felt unloved; he was blessed, yet he felt anything but blessed; he was surrounded by caring people but felt totally alone; he was amid happy people but felt only depressed and sad; and he felt angry, hopeless, and as Christians would rightly say of another who had not embraced the faith, "lost." No two habits exhibited these defeated feelings in Old Joe more than the two often associated with these feelings: his incessant smoking and drinking.

It was late summer that the years' old scenario I have just described would be dramatically altered. Old Joe's and Leah's daily routine of two very different, but conjoined worlds colliding, while attempting to survive within a single home, would be forever changed.

It was amid what Southerners call "dog days" that Leah felt an unusual pain in her lower abdomen, toward her right side. The pain intensified, and she made an emergency visit to the local hospital for treatment. As she had suspected, it was an attack of her appendix.

She was taken to surgery immediately. The surgery was described in medical terms as 'unremarkable" which is the best possible result of any medical procedure. Physicians often use the term "unremarkable" to mean that everything is "normal," no negative result of any kind. I still recall that marvelous day when, following my own surgery for the removal of a kidney cancer, that the doctor said, "I have great news for us all, the surgery was 'unremarkable.'"

All of us who knew and loved Leah that evening rejoiced with her that all was well, and her prognosis was wonderful.

The following day, however, everything related to Leah's health dramatically changed. For totally inexplicable and unanticipated reasons, her heart suddenly stopped beating. She was resuscitated successfully, but her heart simply could not for a long period of time withstand the trauma. The following night, Leah had her visitation and went to forever be with her Lord. When Old Joe was told, for a moment I thought I saw a glimpse of the young Old Joe Leah had so deeply loved.

In that moment, he dropped his head as if to guard against anyone noticing, turned his head aside, and while taking a deep breath brushed his eyes quickly but softly with the back of his hand as if to wipe away any irrepressible tear. Then in a slightly broken voice he muttered, "I'll miss her."

The church was literally filled to its capacity for Leah's funeral, held a couple of days following her death. It was the first, and unknowingly to me at the time, the last occasion I would ever see Old Joe "in church." He sat almost stoically throughout the church service and the subsequent internment service at the cemetery.

As was the custom, following the benediction at the cemetery I shook his hand, which he extended rather matter-of-factly, and expressed again my sympathy. Old Joe then simply stood and, with very few words to the others gathered, walked directly to his pickup truck and left for home.

That night, as I reflected on the events of the day, and particularly remembering how Leah had expressed on more occasions than I could recall, "Every day I pray for Old Joe's salvation," I made a personal commitment to attempt again to befriend Old Joe in hopes that he might be open to Christ's love and redemption. Sometimes death and grief, perhaps just for a moment, jar open even the most fortified resistance.

For that reason, a few days later, I drove to the small fishing community just north of town, located near Sapelo sound, which leads out to the Atlantic Ocean where Old Joe and Leah had lived for decades.

Old Joe was standing in the yard as I pulled into the gravel driveway which afforded a large, open, gravel parking area in front of the small, modest house. I remember almost involuntarily bracing for the greeting, "What in the hell are you doing here? Didn't I tell you I don't want anything to do with that Christianity stuff?"

But I was somewhat pleasantly surprised instead with, no handshake included, "What's on your mind preacher?"

"You are Joe," I said. "I came to do two things. One, I wanted to personally deliver to you this printed copy of Leah's eulogy. I thought that perhaps someday in the future you might wish to reread it as you think of Leah. I know you will miss her…we all will.

"Second, I just wanted you to know that as alone as you must feel, you are not totally alone. I am going to always be as close as your telephone. I would count it a privilege if you find yourself needing a friend, you will allow me to be that friend."

Old Joe momentarily looked down at the ground while scuffing the gravel with the toe of his white rubber fishing boot, then looked up and spoke the first kind words to me I could remember: "Thanks…you are the only person that has come by or offered anything…Thanks."

Following a moment of silence, I asked, "Well, what are you up to?" local jargon meaning, "What are you doing today?"

Old Joe said, "I just thought that I would walk around the property and check on things."

Although Old Joe's statement suggested a large estate, Old Joe owned less than five acres of land. "His property" included only a shed and a small barn easily within sight of the house. His limited acreage was sided toward the ocean by reeds and marshland, separated only by what locals call a "highwater cut." A highwater cut refers to a separation in the marsh which allows open water to reach the shoreline at high tide, an area routinely dry and devoid of any water at low or mean tide. Some highwater cuts on the occasion of high tides provide sufficient depths for the launching and mooring of a boat, provided the boat is either piloted elsewhere or re-trailered before the mean or low tide, lest the boat becomes left aground, something a local would never do.

What I really heard Old Joe saying in response to my question, "What are you up to?" was, "Nothing really. I am just meandering and thinking…I am alone…and I am lost."

"Mind if I walk with you?" I asked, wondering if even that slight jester was too much too fast.

Said Old Joe to my relief, "I don't care." Frankly, two men for the next fifteen to twenty minutes never walked slower to travel less distance without saying a single word than did we. But there was communication, make no mistake about it.

For example, as we proceeded past the barn, which was hardly larger than the nearby shed, I noticed it sheltered a small tractor to one side and a small skiff on the other. The skiff I could easily understand, but the tractor was a mystery. For the life of me, I cannot imagine why Old Joe maintained it, but he did.

Nevertheless, as we stepped away from the tractor and the barn, suddenly what appeared to be a large gray cat emerged from a nearby bush. I was surprised again by what I saw.

The cat, obviously unafraid, walked up to Old Joe. Old Joe, completely out of character with the non-affectionate man I knew, knelt, and began to tenderly stroke the cat. To my further surprise, Old Joe broke our long silence by saying to the cat, "There. There. You'll be okay."

"Your cat?" I asked.

"No," he said, "just a stray. He just showed up here one day. I see him time and again. I think he is like me, just trying to make it another day."

I did not ask Old Joe to explain further at the time. Call it divine inspiration, or what you will, I had the idea that had I pressed the point, our visit would have been instantly over. But I do remember thinking, "I wonder if you were ever able to show Leah even a modicum of the tenderness and love I am watching you extend to that stray cat? I hope so."

After Old Joe stroked the cat a final time and stood, having broken the silence, he added, "Let me show you what I have just built."

Walking around a few trees and a bend in the shoreline, there it was. My first impression of what I saw left me with the same thoughts as the tractor, "Why this? Why here?"

At the other shoreline of this highwater cut was a new, not inexpensive dock, constructed out of the appropriately pressure-treated lumber. On most highwater cuts a dock is not that unusual. However, a highwater cut such as this one and a dock of such expensive construction seemed to be less than reasonable.

You see, I knew, given the length of this highwater cut, this dock would not touch water even on most high tides, perhaps only on two or three "freshets" a year, but I could not imagine much more.

Even then, when the water would reach this dock, the depth would be insufficient to launch any boat, even the small skiff I had seen sheltered in the barn. Why the water would be so shallow there would not even be fish or crab to be caught, much less enough water for swimming or playing. Why would anyone go to the expense of such time, money, sweat, and arduous labor to build this dock in such a place?

I certainly did not ask Old Joe for an answer. I do remember saying, "Fine craftsmanship, Joe. You certainly know how to build."

It was Old Joe's turn to stretch my mind still again. Said he, "I did want to do a good job. That dock will be around a long time, probably longer than you and me." Then he added, "Who knows? The way sandbars move and the way the tides change, and changes things, maybe one day there will be deep water here. Who knows?"

And letting his words drift away with the ocean breeze, he

added in words almost too soft to hear with a wishful but realistic sigh, "Yep, that dock and I have a lot in common."

At that moment one could have knocked me over again with the proverbial feather of unexpected insight. Old Joe, I believe unknowingly, had just revealed his soul to me. Praise be to our Lord I did not miss it.

Death and grief had stirred something in Old Joe. The door to his heart was ajar, again even if only temporarily and ever so slightly, but not closed. And this dock was indeed a metaphor of Old Joe's life, even his hope, however miniscule. "The way things change," he had said, "Maybe someday."

I left wondering that day, "Was Old Joe really talking about the physical water and the dock? Was he talking about himself? Or was it both?"

Over the next few weeks, I seized opportunities to visit Old Joe again and still again. I could sense it. Although we still did not discuss specifically the Christian faith, Old Joe and I were becoming genuine friends who did appreciate our visits together, as brief as they were.

And, yes, I said that we did not specifically discuss the Christian faith. We did not. But that did not mean that our visits were devoid of a Christian witness. Old Joe knew who I was. He knew who I represented. And I was convicted that if I could convince Old Joe that my caring was authentic, he might genuinely believe that Jesus's love was likewise authentic. To this day, I am convinced that such a witness is creditable and made more believable than that of the tract-holstering accuser who demands a cold confrontation on the street, hoping to carve another notch in his or her own Bible cover, although I do admire zealous efforts for our Lord's sake. Note I underscore, "for our Lord's sake."

Well, as the "dog days" passed, the leaves of summer began to change colors, giving way to the bare branches of Fall. But for Old Joe and my relationship with him, it was still spring. Old Joe and I had even been seen sharing a meal at the local restaurant, where all the local politics were transacted and the real "local news" was generated. I can only wonder what news Old Joe and I created. I only know that although we were greeted with polite nods, no one ever asked me how I succeeded in getting Old Joe to dine with me, much less if I thought he might one day come to church.

The calendar turned to October, roughly four months since Leah's death. The day was routine until my secretary informed me that a physician from the nearby hospital wished to speak to me on the telephone. The physician said that he was calling at the wishes of a Mr. Joe Smith to inform me that Mr. Smith had been admitted to the critical care unit of the hospital as the result of sudden chest pains. He further requested that I not visit Old Joe until the following day, explaining that as they were continuing to diagnose his condition, they were also keeping him mildly sedated. However, he fully expected Old Joe to be able to share with me the next morning. I admit that it was with a degree of reluctance that I consented to the doctor's wishes of delaying my visit.

But the next morning, without delay, I made my way to the hospital. I was stunned by Old Joe still again, given what I saw. Old Joe was still in what we call "the critical care unit," although he was not confined to a critical care bed, nor restricted by the multi-faceted IVs and monitors that would be prevalent should I visit someone in a similar condition in a hospital setting today.

Old Joe was sitting in a large patient chair which appeared to be an oversized La-Z-Boy home recliner. He did have one IV and one monitor attached. But most notably, he was enjoying two amenities I had never seen a patient given in a hospital, nor have I seen since.

Old Joe had a smoking cigarette wedged in an ashtray sitting on the serving tray attached to the front of his chair. And he had in his hand a pop-top can of beer.

Before Old Joe ever began to talk to me of his condition, seeing what I have just described to you told me what I was about to hear: Old Joe was dying. The doctors knew it. Old Joe knew it. The cigarette and beer were simply to keep Old Joe comfortable. And, no, he was not intoxicated or even slightly light-headed. The beer and tobacco would avoid any unnecessary pain of withdrawals, but nothing more.

As Old Joe began his story, although similar settings began to emerge within my mind, I noticed there was something different, not peculiar, but different, in Old Joe's demeanor: his tone of voice, his direct gaze. All were pleasantly different.

And rather than just hinting at his real thoughts and feelings as I had learned Old Joe was adroit at doing, or looking down or off to the side, Old Joe looked me squarely in the eye and said, "I was down at the dock, preacher, that dock I built by the house. Remember, I told you that the dock and I had a lot in common. Well, that is what I was thinking about.

"That is when it happened preacher. I heard a voice say, 'You are right. If nothing changes, that dock will never be of any good to anybody…and, Joe, neither will you.' I said to that voice, 'Are you really who I think you are.'

"The voice said, 'Joe, you know who I am!' And preacher, I did know. The Lord was talking to me. And I said to Him, 'But I am old. My life has been a bust, a waste.' But He said that as much as that disappointed Him, and it did, it did not matter now. What mattered was today. He wanted me to say that I would believe Him, follow Him, respect, and love Him today. I said, 'Let me think.'

"I did not hear the voice anymore. I tried to talk to Him, but I did not hear or feel any response. Later my chest began to hurt. Then it was like it all caved in on me and I could not breathe. I called for help. The next thing I remember clearly is being here in bed. My chest did not hurt anymore, but I was hooked up to all this stuff.

"That is when it happened again. I heard the voice again, but this time not only did I hear Him, I saw Him. He was radiant. His eyes looked at me in a way that I knew that nothing was hidden from Him, yet He still cared about me. And he simply said, 'Made up your mind?'

"I said, Yes. Whatever it means, I will follow you. I want things to be different. I want to change. I trust You with it all.

"That is what I did, preacher. And I meant it. I do regret so much, but now I am so glad. I am so glad that everything is okay. It was like I then felt His hand on my shoulder. And He smiled. He said that I was going to be with Him very soon. He said that He would be coming back to get me.

"And, preacher, you should have seen the doctor's face. He looked so troubled, and his voice was sad when he looked at me and said, 'I have some bad news for you.' And I said, bad news? You mean that I am going to die? That is the bad news? It's okay.'

"I do not think he understood. But, preacher, you understand, don't you?" I said, "Yes, Joe. I understand."

Then Old Joe added: "You know, preacher, if anybody should ever ask you to define heaven in one word, I know what the one word is…"

"What is the word?" I asked. And with the gaze of a blind man who is so full of joy because for the first time he can really see, looking me squarely in the eyes, Old Joe said, "The word is 'surprise!' The word for heaven is 'surprise!'

"So many people in heaven are going to be surprised when they see me there. I don't know if Leah will be surprised or not, given that she prayed every day that I would be. But everybody else will be. Why--and he chuckled-- "I am surprised too."

Then with a reflection of dire seriousness, following a brief pause, he added, "Do you know what the other surprise in heaven will be? It will be…who all is not there? Yep. The word for heaven is 'surprise.'"

Old Joe and I continued to visit for a while. And for the first time following a visit with him, I said, "Let me pray with you." He said "Of course!" As I worded our prayer, Old Joe said, "Yes Lord" to every word of praise and petition within the prayer, underscoring the reality of his newly found faith.

It happened as Old Joe said it would. That was the last prayer and visit Old Joe and I would enjoy on this earth. That night, Jesus returned and took Old Joe to heaven and to heaven's surprise.

Having thought of Old Joe's description of heaven as *surprise*, I wonder if that is not what John in his Revelation and the Apostle Paul in his letters were trying to tell us with all their descriptions of "glories" and "wonders"--that heaven itself is going to be full of wonderful surprises beyond the fact of who is, or is not there.

The day I officiated at Old Joe's funeral, I wish I could say that many attended to hear his story. But regrettably, very few attended. Few even noticed, I think, that Old Joe had died. But those who attended heard me tell what I preserved in the written eulogy, which I gave his son. They heard me tell about a dock and a man who had a lot in common…hoping for a day when the tide would change, and the water would rise, and bring with them usefulness and life.

I do not know if the dock that Old Joe built on that high water cut on Sapelo Sound will ever see that day, but, thanks to the Lord Jesus Christ, Old Joe did!

Chapter 6

Kay

The relationship of a pastor and his personal secretary, or ministry assistant, is unusual, to say the least. They deal with different people, circumstances, and confidentialities every day. The specific tasks, judgments, stresses, and professionalism required within such a shared role dictate that ideally the pastor and secretary be friends. I think possibly that is why Jesus once said to His disciples who He called to work with Him, "I no longer call you learners, I now call you friends (see John 15:15, RSV)". Friends can more easily strengthen and encourage each other as they seek to undergird still others.

When I became the senior pastor of the First Baptist Church in the small coastal city of Darien, Georgia, I cannot say that the secretary and I were immediately friends, nor in truth did we pretend to be, as I have known some others to do. We definitively were not enemies, but we simply seemed from day one to discover issues upon which we could disagree.

For instance, office protocol. Having been born in the community and having served well for years within the church, she was much more laid-back than I. She thought that I was too "rigid."

Time would prove that we both had room to grow toward a more agreeable, mutual position where we would both be comfortable. Thank God we did.

Another area of concern was the local government in which she served in an appointed position directly involved with the public. Again, she had served well before I arrived and continued to do so, but she thought I was more given to a greater Georgia ethic than to a specific community ethic. Again, we both had room to grow toward a more agreeable, mutual position, and thank God we did.

Still another area of concern was our children. She was the mother of two fine boys. I was the father of a young son and younger daughter. She thought that I was much too strict as a parent while she thought of herself as much more easy-going and tolerant. I do not know that we ever reached a definitive common page on this one. But as the months turned into years, we came to better understand and support one another's position and all our children.

In fact, not only did we learn to laugh at our differences, we learned to blend them. And this was evidenced in the fact that together we coached our children in the local recreational leagues to several league championships. So as different as we were, we were able to succeed together.

So, you guessed it, Kay and I became devoted friends. I believe our relationship did set an example within the church and community testifying that ministry is always more effective when it is shared. For the successes attained are reciprocally multiplied.

Late May, and early June 1992, was a most special month for Kay and her family. As most parents will attest, it is a day above other days when the first child graduates from high school. It is a day that is accompanied by tears of both undeniable sadness and absolute joy. The parents weep because the nest of the familiar home is about to be disturbed as the child leaves soon for college or vocational training. The child is no longer totally dependent, or at least ideally is not.

But the parents also celebrate. The child has grown and is maturing. At least thus far all is well in their development. And that diploma, once in hand, is more than a piece of parchment symbolizing the child's achievement. It is a testimony of the parents' love, sacrifice, and dreams.

Such was the occasion that late May evening when Kay and her husband witnessed the graduation of their eldest son, with his diploma in one hand and a baseball scholarship in the other, eager to attend a state college in the Fall. We all celebrated, and rightfully so.

The following week, Kay, with a special friend, was excited about continuing her celebration with another of their "shopping adventures" to Savannah, Georgia, a little over an hour away. Such a shopping adventure was not that unusual, but the excitement in this instance was to focus on a special follow-up gift for the graduated elder son.

It was Friday, June 5th. Typically, Friday is the day I would take "time off," although, if the truth is told, the pastor is always on call and technically never off work. But for reasons I do not recall, I was in the office for most of the day.

It was almost lunch time when Kay tapped on my office door, entered, and sat in the wingback chair across from my desk. I noticed the puzzled look on her face and asked, as any friend would, "Kay, what's up?"

As she began to speak, I further noticed that her eyes were

glassy, not to the point of tears but expressing grave concern, almost fear. She said, "Please don't think that I am losing my mind, although I am prone to wonder myself. But just a short while ago in my office something strange happened…," and then pausing she said, "to me."

She explained, "As I was completing the Sunday morning's worship programs, I suddenly felt as if I was not alone, although no one was in the room with me. Also, it was as if someone was trying to tell me something, but I could make no sense out of it. Then, strangest of all, it was if my spirit was uncomfortable in my body. For just a moment I wondered if I was dying, but that thought quickly passed.

"Now I am just wondering what it all means. Is someone, or is my body, just trying to alert me to something? I must admit, it is still a bit frightening to me. I really do not feel physically ill. I am very tired, because the last two weeks have taken a lot out of me. I have a slight headache, but not to the degree that I think I need any medication. What do you think?"

I responded with sheer honesty, "Kay, I do not know what to make of it. You know that it is one of my convictions that a person is always wise to listen to their inner voice. But I do not hear you saying that you received any clear message. I have never felt my spirit attempting to leave my body, so I cannot fully relate to how you must specifically feel. Kay, I am concerned for you, and I am happy to continue to listen and explore this with you, but you asked me, What do I think? I can only affirm again that I am concerned, but I cannot explain it."

Kay continued to describe her awareness of a presence she could not see, and a voice with a message she could not hear. She repeatedly said that she was not certain if it was just her mind or body trying to tell her something rather than some other entity.

It was around 12:30 p.m. when I recall looking at the clock and saying, "Kay, you have told me that in addition to the questions, you have a headache and are extremely tired. I also know that you and Alice are planning your shopping adventure for this weekend. Please do me a favor. Please take the rest of the day off, go home and rest. I will stay in the office, answer the phone, and receive any visitors. I want you to take the rest of the day off and take care of yourself."

"Thank you for caring," she said. "I know you do." But then she added in typical "Kay" fashion, "No, I will go get a sandwich and come back. I am not leaving early."

Then with a playful retort, but sincerely, I said, "Take the rest of the day off and take care of yourself. If you don't, I will fire you," to which she responded, with a smile, "I said 'no!' So, fire me if you will, just consider this my notice." We both chuckled.

Well, you can probably guess who triumphed in that exchange. Following a prayer and her quick sandwich, Kay returned and worked the balance of the day. When she finally called it a day, before leaving for home, she dropped by my office again simply to say, "Thank you," thank you for having listened earlier in the day to her account of the strange occurrence she had experienced in her office. She added with her unique wit, "Thank you also for sincerely caring… I am glad you did not fire me." She did affirm that during the remainder of the day she had experienced nothing further out of the ordinary. But as she left, I knew she was still wondering, as was I, "What did all these things mean?"

It was a typical Friday evening at home with my family until around eight p.m. when the telephone rang. It was one of those ancient models with a rotary dial that hung on the wall and had to be answered without knowing who was calling. Personal cell phones, other than the bag type only found in a few automobiles, were not on the market. And no one then would have imagined, "caller ID" or more unthinkable yet, "Facetime."

The caller was a female who identified herself although I do not recall her name. She said, "I am calling at the request of Ben Watts, husband of Kay Watts. I am a physician on call at the Memorial Hospital in Savannah. Mrs. Watts has been admitted and with the family I would request that you come quickly. She and the family critically need your support."

My response was direct and brief: "I am on my way."

Carol, my wife, and I immediately secured a neighbor to care for our children and traveled to the hospital. As I had been instructed, before going to Kay's room, I checked in at the nursing station where the doctor wished first to explain to me the details of Kay's admission, her condition, and her prognosis.

As I waited only a few minutes for the doctor to arrive, I could only wonder if what Kay had discussed with me earlier that day had any bearing upon the events of the moment.

The doctor was short in stature, petite, polite and most professional. She said, "Dr. Smith, Mrs. Watts was with a friend shopping at a local mall when suddenly she blacked out. She was still unconscious when she arrived at the hospital. We have run tests, and the findings were 'remarkable.'"

Yes, at that moment I felt great anxiety for Kay and her family. For there was that word "remarkable," one with which I had become most familiar.

She explained, "The findings were conclusive. She has contracted a rare form of leukemia. The oxygen level in her blood stream will continue to drop as we do all we can to support her and make her comfortable. It is my belief that she has approximately forty-eight to seventy-two hours before she will expire."

My wife and I looked at each other almost in disbelief. This young mother, not yet forty years of age, who we both had come to respect, love, and admire, someone with no apparent health problems, was now given a life expectancy of only two to three days.

I asked the doctor, "Is she conscious?"

"Yes," said the doctor "She is conscious and able to communicate. Frankly, you will find her now sitting up in the bed. If I had not told you of her condition, you might wonder why we have not dismissed her."

"Does she understand her condition?" I asked. "No." the doctor said. "That is one reason I wanted you here. Her husband told us about your relationship with the family and your experience within the medical community. I attempted to explain her condition to him, but given the shock and trauma he is experiencing, I am not certain he fully understands. Will you go with me to explain to Mrs. Watts her condition?"

With my heavy heart I said, "Of course."

As we entered the room, I found it to be as the doctor had described. Kay was sitting up in the bed, having electronically elevated the head of her bed for back support. She had the expected IV, oxygen supply, and various monitors attached to her.

She, her friend Alice, another friend with whom I was not

acquainted, and Ben were chatting, and there was nothing in their gleeful conversation to reflect the seriousness of Kay's condition. My first thought was, "I think the doctor is right. Ben does not understand."

The mood of the room was quickly altered, however, when the doctor asked everyone, including my wife, to leave the room except for Ben and myself. The doctor spoke only briefly but came to the point, but with one glaring omission.

Basically, the doctor said, "Mrs. Watts, your condition is very serious. Our tests have revealed that you are suffering from a rare and severe form of leukemia. The reason you became unconscious was a drop in your oxygen level which we will continue to monitor and address as the need arises. Obviously, you will be staying with us, and we will do everything to keep you comfortable. We will run further tests in the morning to further clarify possible treatment alternatives."

And with that, the doctor politely said, "Good night."

The glaring omission? The doctor never told Kay or Ben that Kay's prognosis was terminal. Serious? Yes! But not terminal.

After the doctor left the room Ben went immediately down the hall to a small waiting room to welcome the other visitors back into the room. I turned my attention to Kay, who extended to me her hand, saying before I had spoken a word, "I guess today at the office, my body…or someone was trying to tell me something." Then, after a pause, she added, "I am still not certain which, who or exactly what."

I remember masking my own awareness and grief by saying, "I am certain in time we will understand," to which she just smiled.

The other guests returned. It was easy to see that Ben had told them about the diagnosis of leukemia. There was with Kay, most appropriately, shared tears of concern, hugs of affection, and words of support and encouragement. After a while Carol and I both sensed that Kay just needed to rest. We all joined in prayer for Kay as well as for all the doctors, care givers, family, and friends. We said, "Good night" but promptly added, "We will be checking on you in the morning."

And we did. Kay had just finished a light breakfast when we arrived. I noticed that her breathing seemed a bit more labored. Her only comment about it was, "I will be glad when they get this oxygen level adjusted."

It was around nine-thirty a.m. when the doctor came by. Her friendly handshake and warm smile silently affirmed to me that again she seemed glad that I was there. Following her visit, during which she still made no mention of the prognosis of imminent death, she nodded to me as she exited the door.

Reading her body language rightly, I followed her into the hallway. She said, "Nothing I shared with you last evening about her prognosis has changed. Perhaps you noticed her breathing has become more difficult. It will continue to do so. I hope you will stay close by today. By the afternoon I expect significant changes still."

Not knowing exactly what was yet to come, I simply responded, "I will be here."

Not long after I re-entered the room, Kay fell asleep into another much- needed rest. Carol and I went downstairs to the cafeteria for a light brunch.

Returning to the room, we found Kay still asleep. Kay's friend, Alice, had arrived. Upon seeing us and noticing the time, she and

Ben commented that if Carol and I would remain until they returned, they would step downstairs themselves for an early lunch. Of course, we agreed.

But just before they stepped out of the room, Kay awoke. And although her breathing was still labored, I could see by the expression on her face that something significant had taken place. She said to me, "I have something to tell you."

I do not recall if Carol picked up on this, or Alice, who was also a friend of Carol's. But whatever the reason, soon, Carol had joined Alice and Ben as they left the room. Suddenly, I found myself alone by Kay's bedside, listening as she explained.

"I now know what all that meant yesterday in the office. While I was sleeping, or at least my body was sleeping, I was very much awake. Yesterday, it was my body trying to tell me something, but today it was the Lord. Jesus talked with me. He stood right here by this bed and told me not to be afraid any longer. He said that He was in control. He promised that He was going to take care of me. He told me that He loved me. I have always believed He did. But having seen Him and heard Him, now I know He does.

"He told me that I did not need to worry about my family. He loves them, too. He is going to take care of them. Then He told me that my body cannot survive this leukemia. He is going to very soon come again for me and take me on to heaven where later He will bring my family to be with me.

"I want you to tell them, tell everybody, I am with Jesus. I am fine."

"How soon?" I asked, "very soon," she said with a smile.

Ben, Alice, and Carol had been back in the room for only a brief time when it happened. Suddenly, Kay's breathing became much more labored. One of the monitors began to code as the loud alarm sounded, alerting one and all to Kay's distress.

The appropriate personnel rushed us out into the hallway as they sought to again stabilize Kay. Not long into the event, the doctor reappeared and entered the room. Only minutes later, she stepped back into the hallway and called Ben and me aside.

She said, "This is what we anticipated. She needs additional help to breathe, but we cannot any longer simply increase her oxygen supply. She is already maxed. We must relocate her, induce a comma, and place her on a respirator immediately. I do not know how she will respond. You may go with us," she said, again indicating Ben and me.

I knew exactly what the doctor was saying. Kay was dying. Once this coma was induced it would be unlikely that she would ever be conscious again. I also understood that the doctor was saying that if we wanted to say "Good-bye," if we wanted to be with her until her final waking moment, if we wanted to tell her anything, now was the time.

I was amazed that Ben still did not seem to understand what the doctor was saying. For his first remark was, "I will just wait here."

I think I surprised even myself when, almost in a knee-jerk reaction, I said to Ben, "No, you won't! You will walk every step with her. You will hold her hand. You will tell her how much you love her."

Although his first couple of steps resembled those of a man in a crouched stupor, it was as if he suddenly understood. For he straightened up, took her hand, spoke words to her, as by her side they made their way to the intensive care unit. As the devoted husband and fine man I knew him to be, he responded wonderfully.

My last words to Kay? I spoke them to her right there in the hallway. For having seen Ben step up, I felt it inappropriate not to allow the two of them this intimate moment alone. I said to Kay, "I will tolerate no disagreement; take Monday off."

Her response? She shouted to my wife, and they were words laced with the love of a dear friend, "Carol, slap Logan for me!"

The coma was induced. Kay would not awaken from it. A day later, it was as Kay had said. I have no reason to doubt her. Jesus returned and took her to heaven.

Ben would later express his gratitude to me for that wake-up call in the hallway. "I do not think, in spite of all I had been told, that I understood that Kay was dying until then," he said. "I do not think I would have been able to cope had not before they induced her into the coma, she had not had the opportunity to tell me about her visit from the Lord."

Although that was years ago, I can remember thinking at the time, "There is that word again, 'Visitation.' Yes, Kay, too, had a visit from the Lord to reaffirm His presence with her prior to, amid, and beyond the moment of death.

Why do I include her story along with others in this book? Because she, as all the others, brings her own dimension of understanding into this discussion. And in Kay's experience, what different dimension is that? Simply, that of her age.

Unlike all the other individuals whose stories I have recorded thus far, Kay was not advanced in her years. She was still young.

She had no apparent health issues or lingering illnesses. She had not yet traveled though that period known as mid-life. She had no opportunity to experience what is called "anticipatory grief."

Yet, Jesus still came. The Jesus she described was consistent. He was the same Jesus described by all the others who had shared of their "visitation" with me; the personification of love; the warm smile, the penetrating eyes, the tender voice, the reassuring confirmation of joy, peace and life. The response of her heart, soul and faith was also consistent, "Tell everyone that I am fine."

I am grateful Kay and I became genuine friends. I am grateful that we shared the experience of being a brother and sister in Christ. I am even more grateful that I know, thanks to the visitation and my own faith in Jesus Christ, we will always be!

Chapter 7

George Edwards

The next decade of my life witnessed dramatic changes, both personally and professionally, as did the decade before. My children no longer required a child's mentoring, but rather that quality of parenting that would address the needs of late adolescence and early adulthood.

My wife and I would relocate the family to a cluster of small towns in northeast Georgia. I refer to a "cluster of small towns" because the four cities abutted one another, sharing the same city limit posts. But although the four towns shared similar markers and even family ties; they were yet quite different within themselves, a difference that led to more than a few 'political" and "sociological" debates, especially where mayoral influences were concerned.

I was called as the pastor of the First Baptist Church within the largest of the four towns. The church claimed over a thousand members, although on any given Sunday I only saw several hundred of them. Upon being called as the pastor, I was charged specifically with growing the church membership, leading a building program to erect a new educational facility, which was bogged down in highly emotional debate, designing and enlisting a full church staff, and updating the church's methods of administration, including technology, in preparation for the twenty first century.

The church had approved these specific objectives by congregational vote prior to my family's relocation. But I was quick to learn that perceived expectation and implemented expectation are not necessarily the same thing. I can still hear an unhappy church member screaming at me in a committee meeting, "We do not want all these new people in our church. We especially object to them being given leadership roles so soon after they join. They should at least be required to wait a year or two before we allow them to hold important decision-making positions."

I am glad that mentality did not carry the "rule of the day," although it had its lingering fallout. If it had been the prevailing position of the congregation, my tenue would have been short-lived, rather than eventually constituting the longest tenue of any pastor in the history of the one-hundred-years-old-plus church. But that is another book--maybe--on why pastors, their wives and children sometimes cry, and other times rejoice.

But my years in this pastorate, as in the previous ones, had their ups and downs, and thankfully more ups. The lasting friendships that were forged remain invaluable to me to this day.

Given the option, I would accept that pastorate all over again to be a part of what I believe our Lord did accomplish over the years in the lives of so many. All the praise is His!

This new pastorate necessitated constant changes in my pastoral duties. Yes, the pulpit and preaching informed by prodigious study and the pastoral care of the membership remained the number one priority. But in other areas, more delegation of ministerial duties was required as the staff and membership grew, whereupon my role became more and more administrative within the church as well as publicly. It is the "nature of the beast."

Nevertheless, one rule among many remained unchanged. When there was a death, where grief was intense, or where death was anticipated, I was there as I believe every pastor should be.

How many such instances were there? More than I can remember. Wise or not, I did not keep count, as some ministers do. I did preserve numerous eulogies I delivered, but not an exhaustive journal.

I kept no record when I simply read scripture, prayed, or delivered personal remarks while assisting another minister in a funeral service, although I always felt especially humbled, blessed, and honored to do so.

Over the span of years since Kay's death within my previous pastorate, had there been any other instances of visions or visitations shared with me by others preceding their moments of death? Of course. Numerous instances such as those I have already described in the previous chapters of this book occurred, each amazingly similar in detail and all accurate in their understanding of the event. Fred, Harold, Susan, Rachel, and many others could have their stories told, too, underscoring the point that prior to death, Jesus came affirming His love and care for them then and forever.

But for our purpose here, I am convicted that at least still another story must be told in detail. It is the story of a man with whom I quickly became friends upon arriving in Northeast Georgia. Over the years our friendship became so strong that he became in spirit more than a friend. He became my brother. He became the degree of a brother that if in your lifetime you have more than one you probably have had more than your share. I deeply loved him and miss him to this day.

His name was George. He was 35 years my elder. But I never thought of him or consciously related to him as a surrogate grandfather or father. No, he was my brother.

At the time we met, George was semi-retired. I do not think that he ever fully retired, because he needed the company of people that some of his tasks required. That is why whatever his profession had always been, it had been people-centered. George loved people. People loved George.

Another characteristic of George was striking. He was a man of average height, but he was a "big" man physically. That is why he and his wife, Mabel, drove a van from the first day I knew them. George was so physically large that he could not comfortably ride in a car or even in a small truck. He was not flabbily obese, just big. And, yes, there was one obvious reason. Nobody liked Mabel's sweets or biscuits more than he, although I will add my accolades: "They were absolutely delicious!"

I have struggled in my thoughts on how to adequately portray George to the reader. There is just so much to tell. No doubt my struggle is proportionally due to my deep affection for him. So, I hope you will indulge me in this way. What follows is the actual eulogy I delivered at George's funeral, on Sunday, June 13, 2004 at four p.m. at the North Chapel of the Whitfield Funeral Home in Demorest, Georgia.

It is my hope that this memory will enable you to envision and meet the man. In the program I simply referred to the eulogy as the "meditation."

MEDITATION

The author is unknown, although the words of the poet are internationally and timelessly known. Remember the verse?

If you hear a kind word spoken
Of some worthy soul you know,
It may fill his heart with sunshine
If you only tell him so.

If a deed however humble,
Helps you on your way to go
Seek the one whose hand has helped you,
Seek him out and tell him so.

Oh, my sisters and brothers,
As o'er life's rough path you go,
If God's love has saved and kept you,
Do not fail to tell men so!

The poet is right, isn't he? How important it is to tell others how much they mean to you and you care for them as the opportunities arise.

I am glad I did not wait until today to tell George Edwards how much I loved him and how wonderfully blessed I was by him. I am glad so many of you did likewise.

But I cannot help, and perhaps neither can you, on this occasion but to say it again. Perhaps as evidenced by your very presence you are saying, "Me too."

How would I say it speaking for us all? Using an allegory, one day I wanted someone to teach me more than I knew about what love really means. I prayed, "Lord, will you send me Mary? ... The Mary of whom you spoke, saying that she loved most abundantly because she had been forgiven most abundantly, explaining why with the expensive perfume, she anointed your feet and wiped them with her hair. And if not Mary, please send Epaphras, Aquila, or one of those New Testament saints that loved the Apostle Paul through both good times and bad times, easy times and desperate times."

But needing to be taught more about love, God did not send me Mary, or Epaphras, or Aquila, He sent me George. Nobody put it better than you, his family, saying, "Love describes him best."

And it does! Why, single any one of you in the family out and what a story you can tell! Why Mabel, you knew George was full of love when over 62 years ago he fell for you, never to get up. Best of all, he, after falling for you, did not want to get up.

And you children, how blessed you were…to be able to say to me, "He taught us how to be a parent, to be a father, to be a mother. For he never took us anywhere. He never took us to one of our ballgames. He never took us to school activities, proms included. He never took us to church. He never took us anywhere. Rather, he *went* with us. We knew he went with us because he loved us and wanted to be with us. We were important to him."

And you grandchildren, how many games did he play with you? Whether it was Scrabble, word finds (by the clock, of course), Rummy Cue, Go Fish, or some other game to your liking, like seat belt racing, did you not find it strange he never won once, but you always did?

And further, the money he slipped you through your secret handshake with the understood precondition, "Now don't tell your mother or father about this"...And the playful discipline he claimed to others was so stern...telling others, "They will do anything I tell them"...then turning and telling you, "Now go do whatever you want to do." All were his ways of expressing his love for you.

And how he bragged on you, even for the slightest accomplishment. You knew it was love. You were not left to guess. He told you so often. And he always had to be the last one to say it again.

No wonder you all said to me, "We are a 'I love you' family." Of course, you were and are, and I wish other families were. I wish other families had a father who taught them to be like the "Waltons" of television, and say every night before anyone slept, yelling from one bedroom to the other, "I love you, sleep tight."

And the host of us friends... Countless are the times he told us the same thing. In fact, during the last few hours of his consciousness, if he told his physician and me once, he told us a dozen times, "I love you."

I asked the Lord for Mary. I asked the Lord for Epaphras. I asked for Aquila. The Lord instead sent me, and you, George. I am glad He did.

Yet on another day, I asked the Lord to send me Barnabas. On this day, my shoulders were slumped, my feet felt heavy, my spirit was downcast. I needed encouragement. I asked the Lord to send me the New Testament Barnabas, whose very name means "encourager." But the Lord did not send me Barnabas. He sent me George.

He sent me the same George who had a way of putting a smile on my face, of lifting my spirit, even before my circumstances were changed. Believe me George could do that. He could make you laugh sometimes even when he was not trying, and even more if he was.

Like the day he became known as "Tarzan" … Tarzan of Cornelia … and his late friend, Ralph, you said probably welcomed him into heaven by saying, "Hello Tarzan." But given his size, he should have known it was risky for him to try to do what others of you had been doing…to swing on that vine over that river up near Cherokee, North Carolina, only to lose his grip and fall into the river, hoping not to be seen, but he was.

Some folks at Level Grove Baptist Church likely still remember George asking them after church that evening, "Wouldn't you like to have some coconut cake?" But only after following him home did they realize that George wanted some coconut cake, too. But George did not have any coconut cake. And neither did Mabel.

He could make you smile. Sometimes he did have ulterior motives. I mean, how many times did he call you, Holly, to tell you on the sly to call your grandmother and ask the night before, "Are you going to prepare some biscuits in the morning?" Mabel, you did not admit it, but I have an idea you soon caught on that scheme, knowing that George was setting you up to prepare him biscuits instead of toast.

He did it to me. Only a few years ago, he was in Griffin, Georgia, where he went by my father's place of business and asked to see him. He told my father, "I need $500. Logan Smith said if I came by here and asked you for it, you would give it to me." How he laughed as my father in shock had problems responding before finally calling me to check him out. He almost got that money.

But he not only made you and me laugh. Knowing our need of

encouragement, he also told us again and again how much he believed in us and what good work we were doing. Why, if I did not know better, and you did not know better, he would have led us all to believe our middle name was "the best." "How blessed I am," he would say, "to have you, the best." He let us know he really believed it.

I asked our Lord for Barnabas, the encourager. Instead, He gave me George. And I am mighty glad he did.

Then still, another day I needed more. I asked God to send me Solomon. I needed direction. I needed insight. I needed the wisdom of experience. But God did not send me Solomon. He sent me George.

If you never really understood how wise he was, you missed fully knowing him. He was committed to learning. He was committed to education, knowledge, and wisdom. Why, likely there is not another man in the history of Habersham County who helped start in small churches more church training programs than did he. Did you know that?

And amid his work at the prison, he was known as being both wise and fair, especially to the many young boys there. Do you know what they said? "Mr. George taught us what fairness was." And he taught them something else. He taught them something about how to manage their money, but even greater as one inmate confessed, "Mr. George taught us to manage our lives."

What has he taught others of us, in addition to all I have said already? How wise is the person like George who learns the value of every day! Said he to me the same morning he went to sleep, not to awaken, "I think I am going." I asked, "Where are you going." He looked at me and said, "You know. But I would like to hang around one more day."

How often he reaffirmed to me the value of time. How fitting that he did so again and again. Wise is the man and woman who does that.

And wiser still, he knew the value of grace. He knew wisely what the secret of enduring love and encouragement is. It is grace. It is forgiveness. Mabel, it is the best, I think, of all your stories…returning from a Florida trip…you wanting to buy a souvenir for the grandchildren, one of those Florida oranges, not the edible ones, but those playful balls.

George promised to stop amid your journey home. But by the time he would stop there were no more souvenir shops. You were furious! And George knew it. Remembering that small plaque that to this day hangs in your kitchen that says, "A happy marriage is the union of two forgivers," he looked at you and said, "You know what we had better do now?" And when amid the fire and smoke you did not answer, he said, "I think we better hurry home and read that plaque."

That was not as much humor as it was, and is, wisdom.

I asked Jesus to send me Solomon. Instead he sent me George. And I am mighty glad he did.

Then I asked the Lord to send me Paul, and if not Paul, send me Stephen. Send me someone who can further teach me what it means to be a person of solid conviction. But he did not send me Paul or Stephen. He sent me George.

He sent me a man who believed, "For God so loved the world that He gave His only begotten Son, that whosoever believes in Him should not perish but have everlasting life" (John 3:16 RSV).

He sent me a man who believed the Easter Angels, "Why do you seek the living among the dead. He is not here. He is risen." And it is as He said, "Because I live you too will live" (see Luke 24:1ff)."

He sent me a man who, when I asked him last Wednesday morning, "George, have you been talking to Jesus?" He said, "Everyday!" And Mabel, you added "All day!"

The Lord sent me a man who said, "Without Jesus, there is nothing!" And he is right.

He sent me a man who in two words wrote for himself the ultimate wonderful epitaph. They were his very last words on this earth as I had said to George as he fought the sleep he so desperately needed, "George, it is okay to rest".

For then he looked me squarely in the eye. I knew his soul was speaking to my soul. And I understood fully what he meant. He said, "It's okay."

That is what Jesus said. "Put your faith in me. And given all that evil, disease, and time as we know it can do, still it is okay. I will see to it. Because I live you too will live."

And that conviction he held up before others in word and deed. He did it through his spirit, testimony, and acts of service that included everything from his faithful tithes to semi-trailer loads of little boy blue jeans.

I asked for an example of a person of genuine faith and unshakable conviction. I asked for Paul. I asked for Stephen. The Lord gave me George and I am mighty glad he did.

He gave him to you, to me, for a long time. Why I can see and hear him now smiling and reminding us as he did often that he had outlived all those doctors who warned him 30 years ago about his own impending death if he did not change his eating habits.

For all these reasons to which I have alluded until we all get to heaven, and for none of us will it be as long off as we might think, we will miss him.

I do not know how the Lord greeted him the other day before leading him through heaven's gates. Did he say, "Hello, George, Daddy George, Big George, or Tarzan?" I do not know. But I am certain He did say, "Let us go. Well done, my good and faithful servant."

Then as friends and family greeted him, I am certain there were smiles, laughs, happy tears and a lot of ear-thumping going on.

How shall I remember my dear brother most? He was a dear, dear man who for his life could not drive a straight nail, but he knew how to walk the straight and narrow.

Let us pray.

*　*　*

Not too long after George's funeral, Mable called the church office asking that when it was convenient, would I stop by her home for a cup of coffee and a piece of cake. She said she had a question she wished to ask, one that only I could answer. That very afternoon I responded with a visit.

How fitting it was that the cake was coconut. As she served the coffee and the coconut cake, I could not help but grin, thinking about my reference in George's eulogy to her coconut cake, wondering if that reference might have been responsible for it being served.

Her question was simple and forthright. She said that she had been rereading the printed copy of George's eulogy which I had given the family on the day of his funeral, as was my practice with all eulogies, when it occurred to her that I perhaps knew more about George's anticipated and realization of his imminent death than either George or I had previously shared with her. If so, she asked if I would share what I knew with her now?

My answer was, of course, "I will certainly share anything and everything I know." She then pointed to the statements in the printed eulogy about the day of George's death and said, "It seems to me that although the rest of the family and I were praying for George's recovery, he knew for a fact that he was immediately going to die. Did he actually know?"

"Yes. He knew," I said. "In fact," and I used the term I have often used in this book, "he had expressed not one, but two visitations."

"Visitations?" she asked with an inquisitive, furrowed brow and a curious stare. "Yes," and I shared with her what George, I do not believe, was keeping from her and the family, but rather had simply continued to process within himself. Or possibly George was simply loving them by not creating even for one unnecessary day the perception that he was leaving them. That would have been so like him.

But whatever his reasons, it was now most appropriate that Mabel know. So, I shared that George's first visitation had occurred many years ago. Today, I do not remember the specifics, but I do recall that George had on a given occasion become desperately ill. Amid his illness, there was grave concern that George might experience death well before his "three score and ten" years.

But as George shared, one night, literally the eve before he began what the doctor's called a miraculous recovery, Jesus came to him. George said, "Pastor, I think I could have reached out and touched Him. His presence, my vision of Him was as clear and real as is yours as I am speaking to you.

"And I must confess," said he, "part of me wanted to go with Him and He knew it. Had I gone then, everything would have been okay. But a part of me wanted to stay here with Mabel and the children. The Lord said to me that He understood. I asked Him if I might have a little more time on this earth with Mabel and the children that I might witness all of them believing and loving Him as I do.

"The Lord said, 'George, many ask Me for more time and I tell them not to be afraid and to come along, but because you have asked specifically, citing your witness to the children, I am going to allow you for a while to stay. But in time, I will be back for you.'

"Pastor," said George, "I never felt so loved. And since that first visitation, although I still do not want to be separated from my Lord or my family for a single day, I have never feared death nor will I."

Then I related to Mabel, "George's second visitation came on the night before his death. You are right. Although I did not elaborate upon it in his eulogy, when George told me, 'I think I am going,' he went onto explain that Jesus had returned and told him that it was now time to come with Him. The Lord told him that he could come now in the knowledge that his family would follow him and be reunited with him after a while. Knowing this was specifically what George had in mind when he spoke his last words to me as I cited them, 'It's okay.'"

Mabel and I did share more that day than coffee and a piece of coconut cake. We shared some more tears of grief, loss, gratitude, love, faith, and hope. We shared in our love for George, one another, and our Lord, the fulfillment of our Lord's promise of a peace such as this world does not know…His peace…a peace that passes all understanding(see John 14:1ff RSV).

What is so different about George's story? He is one of only two or three among the many who in sharing their experiences with me have addressed the issue of our Lord possibly extending their time on earth for the possibility of the salvation of others, if we dare ask Him honestly and sincerely upon the occasion of His coming.

But that which I find the most comforting from within his story is the confidence and courage with which George faced both life and death. As George said, "When you have seen Jesus, you know in your heart of hearts that it's okay."

It does occur to me that George's story is very similar to that of the Apostle Paul, who said, in essence, having himself seen Jesus, "Whether I go to be with Him or stay here on earth for your sake, it's okay." (see Philippians 1:21ff RSV).

I can only wish that more men on this earth held the faith, lived a life, and even experienced death as did George Edwards!

Chapter 8

John

Not many weeks following the death of my dear friend George, late on a Friday afternoon, an elderly man, a retired medical physician, came to the church office asking to see me. He was a member of the church. At the time we had spent little time together except for the brief greetings at the conclusion of the regularly scheduled worship services he frequently attended.

He had been retired for years. Undoubtedly, he was still highly respected. And yet, as many such people I have known, he had a loneliness about him that over the years I have come more fully to understand. Few people are lonelier than CEOs, chairmen and chairwomen of the board, highly successful individuals, and pastors of large churches.

I suppose the common thought is that given their roles in which they meet and serve so many people, they could not possibly be lonely. However, nothing could be farther from the truth. Although they do interact with numerous individuals, the greater the number, the fewer still seem to risk inviting them into their homes, out to dinner, much less into their personal lives.

I have no idea how many thousands, literally thousands, of

people this retired physician treated. But I became aware, beginning on this Friday afternoon, that few people on a personal level interacted with him outside his wife of many years, his children and their spouses, and a "prized" grandson who literally adored him as "Grandpa" in every way.

After our greeting as he entered my pastor's study, which is the religious jargon for "office," he took a seat in one of the burgundy winged-back chairs across the room from my desk. I took the seat of an identical chair just to the side of an adjacent lampstand.

I could immediately tell that his heart was heavily burdened as our greeting was marked by his downward gaze, stooped shoulders, and low-pitched voice. Normally, he had stood very erect, looked me squarely in the eye, and spoke with an impeccable diction and a strong tenor. But not on this day.

As he righted himself into the chair he unashamedly got directly to the point. "I need help," he said. "And my family needs help, particularly my grandson." He could not contain himself any longer. He began to weep profusely.

In response, I said, "I will weep with you whatever the source of your tears. Take your time and weep for as long as your tears dictate. If God's grace is to be found anywhere, it is in our tears." Then I was quiet. I just leaned forward and rested my hand in reassurance on his shoulder.

After a while, possibly five minutes or longer, he began to recover his voice. Then he continued: "My grandson, who recently celebrated his nineteenth birthday, has for some time been complaining of headaches. Given all the demands that have been upon him, we have all been attributing those headaches to stress.

"Not too long ago he graduated from high school. For him academics have never been easy. He has always been more of a rugged, hands-on, mechanically oriented individual. We knew that achieving his diploma created a great deal of stress for him.

"Also, for several years he has been in love with a young lady who seems to love him equally in return. I have no doubt she does. But she is an academician. So, upon graduation, when he wanted to immediately get married, she said, 'Not now. I want to attend college first.' Not long ago, she left to attend an out-of-state college. Although she did not breakup with him, it has obviously affected their relationship which has weighted heavily upon him.

"Still further, he has started a new job as an automobile mechanic while attending the local vocational school. That has added even more pressure. That is why his mention of headaches along with his heartaches did not wave any red flags. We have been thinking that anyone in his situation would be abnormal if they did not have a headache."

He continued, "But he blacked out while driving about a week ago. Fortunately, he was not alone. He was not on the interstate highway he travels routinely, but on a side road and not traveling very fast. When the man riding with him saw what was happening, he quickly grabbed the steering wheel of the car, and although they did veer off the road and into a ditch, they were not injured by the accident.

"But because he did become unconscious, my grandson was transported to the local hospital. Later, he was transported to the regional hospital in Gainesville. Just today we received the diagnosis, and his prognosis is not good.

"They say that he has a cancerous tumor attached to the base of his brain. Without chemotherapy, he has only months to live. With chemotherapy, although the odds are not good, he could possibly have years to live. But they did tell him that the treatments themselves would be traumatic in their likely side effects. And I know this to be true."

After a pause, which included another gush of tears, he proceeded, "But my grandson suggests that he will not undergo any further treatment. It is as if he has decided to immediately stop living and die. He is not doing anything but sitting and staring out his bedroom window into nowhere. I do not know if he is genuinely a Christian. We have talked about everything else in the world for hours at the time, except faith.

"Pastor, my daughter's family does not attend church anywhere regularly. If I can get their permission for you to come and speak to my grandson, will you go speak with him... with them all? He still lives at home. I know they are all devastated. I know that every member of the family wants him to receive treatment as I do. Will you please speak with them?"

Of course, I agreed. However, little did I foresee the chain of events that would quickly unfold. The physician and I continued our visit for a brief time before we prayed together, and he left the office.

I had some knowledge of the grandson. I had met him a couple of times upon his visits to the church with his grandparents. He was a big, young man. He was not obese, but he was large, standing approximately six feet tall and weighing over two hundred pounds. He was among the other things his grandfather had mentioned, not a super athlete, but a fine high school football player well-suited for his position on the line of scrimmage. This would prove to be a valuable bit of information for our conversation yet to come.

The day following my initial visit with the retired physician, he returned to the office to inform me that he had spoken with the parents of his grandson, and they would be most appreciative if I could visit with both them and the boy, whom I will call John. He then provided me with both a phone number and an address so that I could coordinate a visit.

I responded immediately by phoning the family and setting an appointment time for our visit later that same afternoon. Arriving at the home, after being warmly greeted, or should I say accosted by the family's healthy German shepherd, I was welcomed inside.

I hardly had the occasion to say hello before I was embraced by both the mother and father, who through their own tears began to share their thoughts and feelings. Not all their pain or fear was foreign to me. Only a couple of years prior to our meeting, my teenage son, also an athlete, had developed a strange painful growth atop his left foot.

Upon his examination by our local physician, we were told that he had seen this type of tumor before, and he feared "the worst." He said that he wanted to prepare my wife and me for a possible diagnosis of cancer following the biopsy he had performed. He stated that we would then be more prepared to support our son to whom, only then, the results would be shared.

No second-guessing about it. Those were the longest three days of unfathomable agony my wife and I ever spent as we awaited the doctor's call and the test results. I know that I wept, and hardly slept, asking all the questions only God could ever answer while trying to determine how best to tell my son and support his grief.

My own test results of a malignant cancer years later did not devastate me as did this yet unknown "for certain" diagnosis of my son's condition. My pain was so severe, that even when the results three days later did return with the findings of a non-cancerous growth, a benign tumor, I did not know immediately whether I waited to hug and thank my physician or just punch him in hopes of knocking him cold.

Of course, I kept all these thoughts and feelings to myself, trying to avoid as much psychological transference as possible, something all effective care-givers must do. Yet, I heard them articulated by this mother and father, but with one very different variable: their son's tumor was malignant, and his prognosis was extremely poor. As the grandpa had stated, they reaffirmed, "Without chemotherapy, he only has a few months to live. With chemotherapy, which will be anything but pleasant, possibly…possibly he has much longer to live."

"But, unlike my father, I do not even know how to pray," said the mother. "Why, I am not certain there is even a God. We have never attended church regularly. We do not have a pastor. We do not know how to even begin to talk about such things as death and maybe life beyond. Maybe you can help all of us?"

My conversation remained very limited. Such cathartic moments of sheer honesty are rare indeed. Such moments should never be thwarted, lest the openness to receive insight, healing, direction, and hope from all sources, particularly from our Divine Heavenly Father, The Great Physician, be deterred, brushed aside, or even destroyed.

Of course, I affirmed my on-going support with the assurance, "Having suffered grief within my own family, I believe that faith is an absolute essential! I know that I could not cope without it. We will talk about it. I will share my faith with you as the two of you seek to define and embrace your own.

"But at this moment, I would emphasize this: God understands your feelings, especially the fear and the pain. He understands the anger you must feel and will yet. For God, the Father, experienced death in and through his Son, who was killed also by a cancer, a cancer of the soul called sin, and not even His own, but yours and mine.

"At this moment, it is right that we weep. All these feelings are proper for us to feel. Immediately we will begin to deal with them, but not a day at a time, that is too much. We will work through them, and amid them, just a moment at a time."

With those words, my relationship with this mother and father began. It was our first conversation among many. The conversation would continue for some time. But upon feeling and thinking that the moment was right, I said, "Maybe it is time now that I speak with your son." They agreed.

The father remained seated as the mother stood and led me upstairs. We arrived at his room. The mother knocked on the door. Without waiting for a response, she slowly eased the door open saying, almost tentatively, "John, the preacher is here." I heard a low, almost mumbled response, which I interpreted to mean, "Okay."

The mother then stepped away, nodding her approval as I stepped inside. I found John exactly as he had been described. He was sitting in an office chair, shoved away from his student desk, which was up against the wall, adjacent to a window. He was staring out the window as he said, "Come on in."

In fact, he never turned aside from the window until I said, "Your grandpa and your parents told me that I would find you staring out the window. They said that you really were not looking at anything. I really do not believe that. I believe you are either looking at something or specifically *for* something."

I said nothing more as a brief silence passed. John then turned in his swivel chair, looked at me straight in the eye, and with a gaze laced with fear and great emotional pain said, "You are right. I am trying to see into the future, into the unknown. I do not understand what I am facing or why this is happening to me. The very word 'cancer' scares me. The idea of dying is something that I cannot really accept. Yet, I somehow know it is very real. I do want to live, but I cannot accept what the doctors have told me that chemotherapy is going to force me to endure. I keep thinking, all a few more years will mean is that I am still going to die. Why not, as much as it scares me, just get it over with?

"Yes, I am looking for some answers. Mom and dad simply say they have no answers. Grandpa can hardly speak to me without crying, but what he keeps saying is that I must look for God, but I do not know if I saw God even at this moment that I would recognize Him ... I just keep looking out the window. The answer must be out there somewhere. I don't know, maybe I am even looking for God. I just wish I could see something."

I responded, "John, I cannot say that I know what you are feeling. I have never been told that I have cancer. I have been told on one occasion, due to a very serious infection, that I might not survive. I was in my early twenties at the time, but I still remember weeping and wondering what it all meant, and how it would all work out, not altogether differently from what I think I am hearing you say.

"But no, I cannot say that I know exactly what you are feeling. But if you will allow me, I will look out that window with you, and we can share with each other what we think we see. Together, we will both seek answers. Together we will both seek to find the strength we need and the ease of our pains and fears. Who knows, maybe, together, we ultimately will see God."

John brushed aside a tear from his eyes as he said, "Preacher, I think I would appreciate that." Then and there, the basis for our relationship was established. After listening further to John's story, I sensed that John and I both had begun to tire. As any caregiver knows, such communications, especially listening with what counselor's call "the third ear," can be absolutely exhausting.

But greater still is recognizing that moment of "peak revelation," that moment when ideally every counseling interaction pauses. For if that moment is bypassed by further discussion, the insight of the moment can become quickly dulled, even buried beneath a deluge of other thoughts, or what I call, "unnecessary stuff." I sensed John and I had succeeded in planting one essential thought during our initial conversation. We had at least considered the possibility, "Maybe we will see God."

Before leaving, I asked John if I might say a prayer for us. He said, "Yes." I do remember asking amid the prayer, "Lord, as much as we want to understand, what we want most is to know that you are with us," a petition which John to my astonishment later recalled.

As I opened his bedroom door to leave, John asked, "Could you please come by again tomorrow?" I said, "Of course." I will drop by when I leave the office about five o'clock or so. See you then."

The parents were very gracious and expressed gratitude for

my visit. I shared with them John's request for another visit the following day, which they found reassuring. "Of course, please come," they agreed.

The following afternoon, John was immediately much more congenial with his greeting than the day before, although his position in the office chair was unchanged. As I sat, intentionally in the same position I had assumed the day before, John got straight to the point as to what was foremost on his mind.

"I told you yesterday," he said, "that I could not bear the thought of suffering through the chemotherapy treatments as the doctor described them to me, especially with no guarantee they would do any good. I told you the thought of the side effects of the treatments alone scares me almost more than anything.

"Well, in spite of the fact that my parents and my grandpa want me to accept the chemotherapy treatments for at least a chance of living longer, I have decided to refuse the treatments and die."

There was a long pause before either of us spoke. I sensed that whatever I was about to say would be critical for John. I noticed him slightly leaning towards me as he awaited my response, his body language asking as well as suggesting, "What do you think? Am I right or am I wrong? Should I be content with my conclusion or possibly should I reconsider?"

As I looked into his eyes, it was as if for a moment I felt myself on the outside of that window through which John had continually been gazing. I heard my own inner counselor, whom I believe to be the Holy Spirit, saying to me, "He is looking for God. You are not God. Be careful that you do not assume that role either actively or passively."

I have no doubt that it was under that reality of divine guidance that I said forthrightly, "John, I hear what you are saying. As much as I can, I fully understand. But hear me clearly: I am not God. I cannot tell you what God's perfect will for you is in this specific instance.

"I will share with you what I believe to be true. God is on the side of life. He loves you, and your life is most important to him. I believe this to be true because I believe that Jesus was telling the truth when He said that God sent Him to die for your sins and mine as if you or I were the only person that He had ever loved and gifted with life so that we might forever live. (see John 3:16ff RSV).

"I believe that the ultimate reason for such love was, and is, that God desires for us to experience the life He has given to us, even beyond this world, with Him. Life is so ultimately important to God, and because we are made in the image of God, that is why it is so important to us.

"But within our own power to decide, how long should we spend on this earth given a situation such as you have been given? Truthfully, I do not know. But I will ask you before you reach your final decision to consider a couple of things.

"First, what does your prognosis really mean? I think it means, that you might, and I use the word 'might,' you might if you believe in Christ as your Savior and Lord, you might get to heaven before I do. For neither of us, nor anyone else, for that matter, has a guarantee of another year or day or even breath. Why, at best, the idea of another tomorrow on this earth is but a hope and a prayer on our part. If it is not disease that threatens us, what else might happen to cause our death? Why there are more possibilities than you or I can fathom such as natural disasters, car accidents, plane crashes, people trying to do us harm, you name it. So, in one sense, you 'might' get to heaven before I do. But believe me, in saying that, I am not belittling or trying to make light of what the doctor has told you, or any of your thoughts or feelings.

"But another thing, I heard your grandpa, your parents, and you say, and rightly so, that chemotherapy has a great number of possible negative side effects. Possibly like you, I have seen them experienced by others and know them to be real. I heard you say that such treatment brings with it no guarantees. Of course, I know this also to be true.

"But what I have not really heard emphasized, rather only mentioned almost as an aside, is its real possibilities? Although negative perceptions have value, are they always really that helpful? Is the mere thought of a positive possibility worthy of further consideration?

"John, I know that in high school you were a football player, right?"

"Yes," said John, "I was a starter on the line for two years. I played right guard, and even a little tight end, from time to time. I really enjoyed it. If there was anything about graduating from high school that I did not like, it was the fact that I could not play football anymore."

"Well, John, did you win all of your games?" I asked.

"Of course not," he said. "We won our share, although I wish we had won more."

"Did you lose any games you should have won?" I continued.

"Who hasn't?" he said. "I can think of several games, especially one playoff game, that we should have won but let slip away."

"Well, John," I said, "one more question, and do not answer me too quickly. Rather think about it. Did you ever win some games that, given all the odds, you should have lost? I ask you this because I was an athlete in high school, too. My sport was not football, but basketball. But the principle is the same. The games I especially have in mind are those in which I and the team came out eager to play. But before we knew what hit us, we were so far behind in the very first quarter that, if the truth was told, it appeared to make no sense for us to keep playing.

"Why, it would have seemed merciful for the referees not only to have called 'time out,' but 'time over.' Nevertheless, my coach did not quit. My teammates did not quit. And most important to me, I did not quit. As challenging as the circumstances were, including the boos and nay-sayers in the stands yelling for us to give it all up and go home, we continued to run every play we knew with every ounce of strength and energy we had left.

"Then suddenly, as the middle of the fourth quarter rolled around, we realized that somehow we had gotten back into the game. By the time the final horn sounded, by nothing less than a miracle, we had won!

"John," I asked while looking squarely into his eyes, "Did you ever win a ballgame like that?"

He answered almost immediately, "Yes. It is one of the games I remember most."

"Of course, it is!" I said. "Miracles like that do not happen every day on the football field or the basketball court, but they do happen! This is what I want you to think about. Those miracle ballgames would have never happened, if you or I and the team had decided in the first quarter no longer to try, to simply go ahead and lose"…and I paused before adding, "to lay down and die!"

It was easy to discern that John understood my analogy. But to leave no room for misunderstanding, I said, "John, I repeat, I am not God, and I am not wise enough to tell you that I can look into God's mind and know what His perfect will for you here and now is. I cannot tell you that if I were in your place, I would accept the chemotherapy treatments or not, much less apply the terms, 'right' and 'wrong.'

"But I emphasize again that God is for life, and you can take comfort and put your hope in that. I do not minimize, in the least, your struggle. But could this be possible? Could it be that as far as your cancer is concerned, you are still in the first quarter? Could it be that when the fourth quarter comes around you might be one of those who improve the survival rates for others who share your disease? Are you really prepared to call the game now?

"I know there are no guarantees that I, your physicians, family, or anyone else can give you that if you take the treatments you will live a long life. But maybe…maybe that is not the most important criteria upon which to make your decision. Perhaps the more important decision for you, given the athlete you are, is not 'if' you live, but given however long you may have yet to live, 'how.' How will I live? And if I die, will I do so passively giving-up, or will I fight this disease with my eyes still focused on living?

"It does seem that you are still early in the game. For that reason, I urge you to reconsider whether there is more of the game yet to be played. I know that your decision is one that must be made quickly. I know it is critical. I understand that. But ask yourself, and prayerfully ask your Heavenly Father, if the game of your life here is really over?"

There was silence. It was another of those poignant moments when he finally responded, "I have not thought about it like that. I need time to rethink it."

I knew it was time to say good-bye. And following a prayer for wisdom for us all, I did.

I intentionally did not visit or phone John the following day. In no way did I want to further impose my own thoughts and ideas upon him. Whatever decision he chose, I knew that the decision needed to be entirely his.

Several days passed before the mother phoned and said, "John wants to see you. We all do." At her suggested time, without hesitation, I made my way again to their home.

I became aware immediately this visit would be strikingly different from the previous ones. In fact, John, rather than his parents, met me at the front door. He did something he had not done before, which to a degree surprised me. He immediately stepped forward and gave me a warm, brotherly embrace. It was an embrace such as a friend gives to another after being finally reunited following an elongated separation.

He said, "Come in preacher." There in the living room sat his father, his mother, and grandpa.

He explained, "I wanted to tell everybody at the same time what I have decided." So instead of making my way upstairs as had become my custom, I simply sat down on a love seat next to grandpa.

John proceeded, "Preacher, I have thought a lot about those

ballgames we talked about. I believe you are right. For me, it is still too early to quit and give up. Mom…Dad…grandpa…I have decided to take the chemotherapy treatments. I am going to do all I can to defeat this cancer."

John did not get any further before his mother literally sprang from her seat on the couch and grabbed him around the neck with an embrace that only a mother who deeply loves genuinely can. His words were almost squelched by the uncontrolled flooding of tears and the reaffirmation, "I am so glad, son. I am so glad. I will be with you, every day…all the way."

The father and grandpa allowed the mother and son their moment, but they were not far behind with their hugs, embraces, kisses and words of encouragement and affirmation.

After some time, as the moment became again composed and settled, John said, "But I have something else to share." Given the moment, no one could imagine more important or greater, happier, news. But from my perspective, and Grandpa's, indeed it was. Said John, "Preacher, I reached my decision not only by just thinking, but as you suggested by trying to pray, although I am still not certain I know how to pray. But I do know that as I tried to pray, I got the feeling that God really was listening. I do not think I have ever had that feeling before.

"Preacher, I want to be a Christian like Grandpa, like you. Mother and dad, I want you to become Christians, too. As I go through the treatments, I want us all to pray together. I want us to share that same feeling that I have already had.

"Preacher," asked he, "Will you tell me how to know that I am a Christian, right now? Will you tell us all?"

If there was ever held a genuine worship service, it was held right then and there. No words of invocation were ever more fitting or apropos than were John's. The Holy Spirit was undeniably present.

How grateful I was that it was my custom to carry in the inside pocket of my suit a New Testament. Reading from the scriptures, I walked us all down what Christians have long called, "The Roman Road to Salvation."

First, we acknowledged the reality of the presence of sin in all our lives. The biblical book of Romans puts it succinctly, "As it is written, 'none is righteous, no not one…since all have sinned and fallen short of the Glory of God…the wages of sin is death'"(3:10, 3:23, 6:23 RSV).

After I read this, not one of us could or would challenge it. We knew it to be true. If to be sinless is to be perfect, as God is perfect, and it is, not one of us could claim to be perfect either in our thoughts or actions. Nor in the future would we be. That being true, each of us as an individual knew that our own death, both physically and spiritually was deserved and inevitable, like wages that must be paid.

Then, secondly, we acknowledged that our only hope was in the person of Jesus Christ. We read further from Romans, "but the free gift of God is eternal life in Christ Jesus our Lord…God shows His love for us in that while we were yet sinners, Christ died for us" (6:2b, 5:8 RSV).

No. We could never be perfect. We knew that. Yet, here were sacred words of scriptural revelation telling us that Jesus was perfect even in our behalf. He lived a sinless life and died for us, and for us alone. He had no inherent need within Himself to do so other than His love for us and the Heavenly Father. He received the wages of our sins and paid them in full at the cost of His own sacrificial blood. He did for us what we, given our imperfections, could not do for ourselves.

As this truth sank into the consciousness of each of us in the room, we felt the weight of it, the penetrating truth of it, the unfathomable mystery of it, and the existential and very personal call of it. I do not think there was one of us that did not feel our heart beating heavily or have our eyes moistened by our tears. Of course, those we call "old time Christians" have a very succinct and accurate way of describing our experience. "The conviction of the Holy Spirit," they say. And indeed it was.

But no one, or anyone's situation, is changed by mere insight or conviction alone. Therefore, we continued to read from Romans, seeking to further understand perhaps the greatest question of all. What would our response to the love, the sacrifice, the person of Jesus be for His gift of salvation and life offered to us?

We read, also from Romans, the response God desires from us all: "If you confess with your lips that Jesus is Lord and believe in your heart that God raised Him from the dead, you will be saved (from death)… for anyone who calls upon the name of the Lord will be saved." (10:9-10; 10:13 RSV).

John without hesitation said, "I believe." John's parents followed with what I believe was equal sincerity, saying almost in unison, "I believe." Grandpa and I reaffirmed what we had professed years earlier, "We believe too," adding, "and nothing brings us more joy than knowing that we all now share that unique relationship that Christians alone share with other Christians."

Then I read one further affirmation from Romans as an act of celebration as now we all faced the unknown together with Christ and as Holy Scripture affirms, in Christ. "Therefore, since we are justified by faith, we have peace with God through our Lord Jesus Christ. Through Him we have obtained access to His grace in which we stand, and we rejoice in our hope of sharing the Glory of God…(For) there is therefore no condemnation for those who are in Christ Jesus" (5:1-2, 8:1 RSV).

John could not have worded a more fitting prayer of benediction to this most sacred experience of worship. "I do not think I will ever look out my window and see nothing again," he said. "At this moment, somehow, I know that whatever happens, it is going to be okay. I am really…I am really not alone."

John and his parents made a public testimony of their newly found faith the following Sunday as they joined the church which the family of John's father had over the years attended. Soon thereafter, they were all baptized together and received into the full fellowship of that church.

Their new pastor was a fine older man who provided marvelous pastoral care to them as the future unfolded. I would remain one care-giver among many to the family, but never usurping, rather always encouraging their pastor's role. As I reflect, it was good that all of us were reaching out to John and his family, for they would indeed need us all.

John began his treatments almost immediately. The side effects were as expected. As I recall, the nausea, diarrhea and vomiting manifested themselves almost immediately. Other side effects such as hair loss, mouth sores, and loss of appetite were more gradual. As the doctors had foreseen, this healthy-appearing, giant of a young man with a sculptured athletic body, soon began to deteriorate.

His body became more and more fragile. He would easily bruise when he lost his balance and bumped into anything, something that became a frequent occurrence. It became all the more important for all of us as the months passed to guard against exposing John to any infections, not only those we might have contracted, but simply might have carried as his immune system became all the more problematic.

But one area of John's identity remained remarkably unchanged by this insidious cancer and the horrendous side effects of its treatment. His faith in his Lord Jesus Christ remained strong, even strengthened. He would constantly remind us all, "The Lord has this. No matter what happens … it's okay."

Yet all of us who knew him and cared for him suffered, as did he. We all to varying degrees felt his pain and, in our own ways, wept with him and for him.

Now I know that a part of me believes that no one grieves for a child more than a parent. Having lost a child, I know. But there is another part of me that knows what it is to love as a grandfather. That love, too, is deep and unfathomable. It is impossible for me to verbalize its reality orally or to document it accurately in print.

That is why I will risk suggesting that no one grieved more for John than his beloved grandpa, to whom he had been so existentially connected since birth. Although Grandpa's greatest desire for a heavenly promise of eternal life with his beloved family had been assured by John's having become an authentic believer, none-the-less, Grandpa wept. I literally held him in my arms as his aged, frail body shook as he grasped for air between his sobs and gushes of grief.

Perhaps I was too focused upon John to notice the full impact of the grief upon grandpa himself. That is why perhaps I was as shocked as John and the rest of the family when the unthinkable happened.

About nine or ten months into John's treatments, I received a call to come quickly to the emergency room of the nearby hospital in Gainesville, Georgia. Grandpa had been rushed to their coronary center with severe chest pains. Upon arriving, I was escorted by a nurse to an aside room where the family had been gathered for their greater privacy.

Having visited this room before, I knew before I entered what had happened. Grandpa had suffered an acute heart attack and had died almost immediately after arriving at the medical center.

The family had already been told of his death before I entered the room. Among the family members gathered were John and his parents. To this day I have few words for such a moment. Sometimes words are just inadequate…not enough. Therefore, we just embraced one another. We held one another's hand. Without saying a word for a while, we all prayed.

After a while, though, various family members did begin to speak. As the shock and numbness began to ease, it was John who finally asked, "Preacher, would you lead us in prayer?" I do not remember how I worded the prayer, but I have no doubt for what I prayed: for strength, comfort, meaning and hope. I know that I asked what I continue to this day to prayerfully petition amid such challenging grievous circumstances, "Lord may the faith to which we have held, now hold on to us."

John's pastor would most fittingly assist me in officiating at "Grandpa's" funeral. I was surprised that though well attended, the church was not as packed by friends of the deceased and family as it often was on such occasions. Possibly, as with every passing day of my own aging process, I become more fully able to understand. Grandpa had outlived most of his friends and patients. But I was thankful that John was physically able to attend. In fact, I am certain it would have required nothing less than his own death to have kept him away.

Following grandpa's death, John began to talk more openly about his own. In fact, I still remember, vividly, as I sat beside John's bedside on one of his "not so good" days, John saying, "Grandpa was always looking out for me. No matter what happened, grandpa seemed always a step ahead taking care of me. I wonder…I wonder if he went on to heaven when he did to teach me not to be afraid and to help Jesus get my place ready?"

However, when John said this, it was more than apparent that he was not resigning in his battle to defeat cancer. In fact, if anything, I noticed a greater resolve to live because "Grandpa wanted me to live," he said.

But heaven did become a place that became more real to John. It became a reality, a place, much easier to contemplate and envision, and one much less to be feared.

As still more months passed, the news from the doctors at times seemed very hopeful only to subside again into the more probable. For a brief while, the term remission became the word of the day. But one needed only to take a long look at John to know that John was literally being devoured by both the disease and its treatment.

I do not recall anyone given John's condition who survived longer, or, given the analogy he and I used from the beginning, one who fought to win the game harder.

But far too soon, John's health had deteriorated to the point the he spent only a brief time each day out of bed. Even then, he had to be helped, or rather placed, in a chair by a caregiver. He could not alone, without great risk, reposition himself. But the task of lovingly assisting him in doing so was not so difficult. John's size and weight were mere fractions of what they had once been.

It was shortly after John's twenty-first birthday that my ministerial assistant--we called her a secretary in those days--forwarded me the message that John's parents had telephoned. The message read, "They said that John wants to see you as soon as possible. They sounded as if the situation was urgent."

Do not ask me how I knew, but I did know. It was urgent. I immediately left the office and speedily made my way to John's home. As they had done countless times over the last year, or year and a half, John's parents met me at the door.

They said, "We have just put John in his chair for a brief while. He is not as upset as we are. But we sense that something is happening and although we cannot say that we understand it, the spirit of it all is frightening us. When John said that he needed to talk to you now, we felt that he meant as soon as possible. Your secretary called to tell us that you were on your way. He is expecting you."

They did not accompany me upstairs to his room. That formality was no longer necessary or expected. I knew that I had become a member of the family. I tapped on the door, and John responded with a "Come on in."

What was John doing? Perhaps you can guess. Except for his physical appearance and a relaxed expression on his face, the scene was actually the same as it had been on that very first occasion I had visited John to discuss his recent diagnosis and refusal to receive any medical treatment.

John was looking out the window. The relaxed expression on his face did suggest, however, that now he was no longer staring at nothingness, a pain riddled future or even a foreboding death. So it was nothing less than what some people call "instinct," but what I believe to this day was the leadership of the Holy Spirit that prompted me with no routine words of greeting to ask, "What do you see?"

Whereupon John turned his face toward me, looked me squarely in the eye, and said with a tenor of utter peace in his voice, "I am looking at heaven. But I wanted to see you as soon as possible to tell you, not about my vision of heaven, but about a visit I experienced in the wee hours of this morning. At first, I thought to myself that I must still be asleep and dreaming. I am sure you have had that experience, too. But then I realized I was very much awake.

"I first noticed Grandpa. He was standing by my bed. I did not try to reach out and touch him or hug him as I would always do. Somehow, I knew I could not or should not. Then I saw the other person with him. Jesus was with him. Jesus told me that I still had no need to be afraid and that soon I will be with Him. I will be fine. And I could not help but notice grandpa nodding his head in agreement as Jesus spoke."

John paused. Giving him a moment to catch his breath and noticing that he was feeling a significant wave of emotion, I finally broke the silence. "So, you will be fine?" I said.

Then he continued as if he had not missed a word. "Yes, I will be fine. I win!

"Jesus told me that not today, but tomorrow, He will come for me. And I will go with Him to heaven where I will be reunited with Grandpa, my other grandma, others who have loved me and who I have loved, and a whole new family of Christian brothers and sisters I will have an eternity to get to know.

"He also told me not to worry about my family, friends, you and others, I will be leaving behind. All of you will be coming eventually. Preacher, I wanted you to know that we all are going to be okay! I want you to tell everybody that!

"Promise?" he asked.

"I promise," I said. And we embraced as only Christian brothers can--a young brother encouraging in the face of his own death, an elder brother over twice his age.

I did ask John if he had told his parents of his vision and his visit. He said, "No, not yet." He said that he would wait and share it, if He could, at the very last moments before his departure. He said that his reasoning was that if he told his parents, they might doubt him, or worse still, believe him and start telling everyone creating a flood of attention and a multitude of questions he did not desire to answer.

"Besides," he said, "although I know my parents believe as I do, and Jesus said that they would be alright, I do not want them to panic, or just sit by my side every second until Jesus comes. I love them. I will miss them. But none of us need that. So, if I have the moment, and believe it to be the right moment, I will tell them."

Respecting John's wishes, I did not tell his parents of his experience. I did assure them after my visit that John was not troubled but at peace, experiencing that peace of which Jesus spoke when

He said, "My peace I give you…a peace the world doesn't understand nor can give" (John 14:27 personal translation). I did tell them to be assured that Jesus extended the same peace to them. They had no need to be afraid.

I did suggest that they spend some additional time with John later in the day just talking about their thoughts and feelings. I knew that such a conversation might afford John that "moment" he was anticipating. Following a prayer with John's parents, I left thinking, "I do not know what tomorrow will bring. But I have heard almost the identical words John spoke before." But this was absolutely the first occasion when anyone telling me of their visitation by Jesus shared that anyone else accompanied Him.

What happened the following day? When his parents went to check on John the next morning, they discovered that indeed Jesus had come for him as John had told me He would. Had John found the moment to tell his parents about the visitation of Jesus and Grandpa? I use the word, but only from my point of view and claiming no innate wisdom on the matter, "Regrettably, No!" Although the parents, before John went to sleep his last night on this earth, had sat beside his bed and had what they called, "a deep, meaningful time of sharing together," John did not share with them his visitation.

Prior to John's funeral in which I assisted John's pastor, who delivered a beautiful and most appropriate eulogy, John's parents did say to me that they thought John knew his death was imminent. I felt it appropriate then to say, "Yes, he did," after which I shared with them what I have now shared with you.

They thanked me. But I only wish John himself had told them. Yet I could see that they were indeed telling me the truth when they said, "That vision makes this bearable. It explains to us why John kept saying, 'Mom, Dad, everything is okay.'"

John's story, as the others in this book, affirms for us all, with the added dimension of loved ones never lost or forgotten, that although we live in a world where so much is not okay, we all as Christians are and will be okay!

But what more does it affirm? Next chapter.

Part Two
Anticipating

*Death is nothing else but going home to God,
The bond of love will be unbroken for all eternity.*

— Mother Teresa

Chapter 9

Two Irrefutable Conclusions

It has been nearly two decades since I delivered John's eulogy. If as a reader you have been counting, you are right. That means the year according to the calendar is 2020. You might have realized this, too: my hair is no longer dark brown or even peppered with gray. It is dominantly white with only a grayish tint.

Yes, I am called "retired," although I still preach, teach and extend personal care at every opportunity, which includes continuing to counsel the grieving, hurt and afraid…all too common experiences within my extended circles of concerns, particularly at this juncture of my life and experience.

Did I pastor and serve other churches I have not mentioned thus far in this writing? Yes. Did I experience other occasions like the few I have detailed in previous chapters? Indeed, I did and continue to do so.

Why do I not write of still another? My limiting of the stories to the few you have read is intentional for several reasons. Your time and the allotted number of pages of this manuscript are one concern, of course. Further, I do not want the reading of these stories to become monotonous to the degree that the significance of the common threads of information contained within them become dulled, confused, or overlooked.

Another concern is that of mere repetition. Every story I have related thus far has included an added perspective, an additional insight, unique to itself. Perhaps you have already picked up on this: not only do the ages of the people of whom I have written vary, but they have been both male and female, younger and older, close and not-so-close relationships, and of varied vocations, economic advantages and academic achievements. This emphasis on diversity is intentional. It is the diversity of the people whose stories I have told that makes their common testimonies so relevant. As diverse as the lives and their stories have been, their insights, their experiences, consistently replicate one another and therefore stand out more prominently. Their differences defy any simple explanation of their common testimonies based merely upon medical research, scientific observation, sociological influence, or psychological transference on the part of me as the writer or you as the reader. This awareness of diversity might be unintentionally masked if too many similar stories were cited.

Still another concern is that of my desire to refrain from even passively sounding as if I wish foremost to write my own autobiography rather than to remain focused upon my originally stated intent: To discuss what happens at the moment of a person's death, specifically, a Christian's death, in hopes that as Christians we all might be reassured, comforted, and calmed; and that any reader who is not of the Christian faith might be influenced to reconsider Christ and ultimately confess Him as Lord. Snippets of my story have had to be told to provide a context for the stories of the individuals cited. But may my Lord Jesus Christ forgive me if any other than He, has been or yet shall be, the person of ultimate focus.

Other concerns? Yes, but I need not elaborate on them here. Another time and place perhaps. Now it is time. It is time to ask, "Given the experiences cited and the insight given by those involved, what do I, and what might we, make of all this?"

No single observation is more significant than this one: Christians do not die as do others who are not of the faith. Individuals who have either denied or simply ignored the faith, never expressing even a hint as to their acceptance of Christ as Savior and Lord, in spite of my witness at the moment of their death, have with varying degrees of anxiety described the experience using the often historically repeated metaphors of "darkness" and "coldness." A significant number of other individuals not of the Christian faith have described an experience of drifting into a state of loneliness, fearfully making comments like, "Oh no, I am losing my grip (on consciousness and life); is anybody there?"

But I have never known a Christian at the moment of their death to speak in terms of darkness, coldness, and loneliness. Rather, they have all spoken to me of a presence. So, to begin with, my observation is that Christians, unlike those people who are not of the Christian faith, simply do not die alone!

This truth is, has proven to be, and shall continue to be a great comfort to many of us. For example, some time ago, I had the opportunity on a Friday evening to visit the Aurora Theater in Lawrenceville, Georgia. That evening was one of nearly one hundred consecutive sold-out performances that spanned several weeks of the epic Victor Hugo musical, "Les Miserables."

Most significant to me was the lead role of Jean Valjean, that of a French peasant seeking his soul's redemption after serving nineteen years in jail for having stolen a loaf of bread for his sister's starving child.

I had the privilege of seeing "Les Miserables" performed on stage in London, England, some years before. As marvelous an experience as that was, and believe me it was, it would not surpass the performance in Lawrenceville. The primary reason was that the lead role was being played by my son, Bryant, who was widely recognized and awarded for his performance.

I had watched my son perform professionally in various roles over the years in theaters in the Southern United States, as well as in New York, where he resided for some years. But this role was different for two reasons. One reason was that it was his dream role. Any father who loves his child finds great satisfaction in seeing his child's dream fulfilled.

Another reason was much more deeply rooted in my own circumstance. Recently I had been diagnosed with a dangerous aneurism in my aorta and warned by the physicians immediately to alter my lifestyle. Although I had been advised about a most dangerous surgery, but with a good prognosis, nothing was certain. Perhaps no one except another individual who has been given such a diagnosis can fully understand the depth of introspection that takes place when one's mortality is stripped of its facade.

Two scenes within the play, "Les Miserables", literally cut into those depths, bringing tears to my eyes. Although I had long understood the theatrical axiom of the ideal of "suspended disbelief," I could not help but see myself in the aged character of my son as Jean Valjean.

When he sang in act two the song, "Bring Him Home", I felt my inner being tense. "Bring Him Home" is a prayer. It begins with the plea, "God on High, hear my prayer. In my need you have always been there…" It proceeds with a petitioning of God to spare the life of the young man his adopted daughter and only child deeply loves and hopes to marry from being killed the following morning amid the carnage of the French Revolution.

I remember thinking how I yet hoped to see my children's and grandchildren's lives unfold. I remember literally praying for myself. "God on High, hear my prayer…In my need you have always been there…grant me more time with them now."

The second scene was at the end of the story. The young man was spared. He and the beloved daughter were married. But Jean Valjean had not been able to attend the wedding. He had been away. Now he was dying, and he was praying again.

But this time, instead of praying, "Bring Him Home," he was praying, "God on High, take me home." And although Jean Valjean's vision of heaven was most fitting, and he wanted to go there, in the stage adaptation of the story amid his prayer, the daughter and son-in-law arrived on the scene pleading with him, instead of leaving for heaven, to stay with them. And he promised to try to stay, although he did die and was received by numerous friends in heaven as the play ended.

Again, I saw myself in the aged character of my son. I realized for a second time that Jean Valjean's story was similar with my story, especially as he prayed concerning how blessed he had been to know the love of a child. I felt at that moment only the deepest love for my wife and my family. I wanted only to embrace them, not ever to leave them. So, yes, again my eyes were filled with tears.

I felt the tears trickling down my cheek when suddenly it happened. Had my wife been able to have been with me that evening, likely the stranger next to me would have never asked. But it was a middle-aged woman accompanied by her adult daughter who, as we stood with the rest of the house to give the company of actors a standing ovation, noticed my silent tears.

She simply asked, "Are you alright?" I was very honest with this stranger. I said, "I am sorry if I have to any degree frightened you. You see, the man playing Jean Valjean is my son. Seeing him literally aged by the makeup he is wearing, I feel like I am looking in the mirror," at which point she interrupted, "My word, you are right! You would almost pass as twin brothers."

I could not help but give a faint chuckle, but added, "Recently I was diagnosed with a most serious illness. I do not know what it means for my future. I could see myself, believing in Heaven, trusting Jesus Christ as my Savior and Lord, looking into heaven, and yet I must confess, feeling the pain of leaving him, his mother, his sister, my son-in-law and grandchildren.

"As wonderful as heaven will be, I felt more like Louis Armstrong than the Apostle Paul, hearing old Satchmo sing with that broad, contagious smile of his, 'It's a Wonderful World.'"

Then I noticed tears beginning to flow from her eyes, and I said, "Oh please do not weep. I did not intend to make you sad. I am okay."

She said, "Mister, you do not understand. I am not weeping for you. I am weeping for me."

Suddenly, the ovation was over. The cast began to exit the stage as the audience began to leave the theater. However, the woman and her daughter, rather than exit, sat back down for a moment. I realized then they both were troubled.

So, I, too, hesitated. I said, "You expressed concern for me. I am a Christian minister. Now I am concerned for you. Why do you weep?"

She said, "I, too, was moved by the death scene of Jean Valjean. But for a different reason. The writer of the play wrote that scene as it should be. No parent should out-live their child, and the family should be together when death comes. No one should die alone."

Having said this, she momentarily experienced a deluge of tears as did her daughter, who embraced her. After a few moments, she added, "But I have outlived my son." Then she became specific in her detailed explanation: "He was only 18 years of age." She named the day of the week. She named the recent calendar day, month, and year. She noted the exact time of night and the address of the accident.

She shared how her son had gone out for the evening with friends as teenagers do. But on the way home the car in which her son was riding left the highway and crashed. As far as the authorities could tell, he was killed instantly.

Said she, "I am a Christian. I believe in heaven, too. He was a Christian. But I was not there. I did not have a chance to tell him goodbye, or not to be afraid. I did not get to tell him one last time how much I loved him. My son died alone." Then she said most emphatically, "Nobody should die alone."

Giving her a moment to catch her breath, I said to her, "But he did not die alone."

She asked almost in a tone of disbelief, "You really believe that?"

"Yes," I responded, "and I will tell you why." Then I shared not only a couple of the stories I have already written in this book, but a biblical basis which I will yet share to validate my conviction. I saw nothing less than a miracle occur.

As I shared, I watched the very countenance of this woman change as she soaked up every word like hot desert sands soaking up a long-awaited rain. In response, she said, "It never occurred to me that a Christian never dies alone. It will not heal the hole that for the rest of my life will daily be felt in my heart, but it does bring to me a great release of guilt and comfort to know that I did not fail my son for not being there when he needed me most."

"No," I repeated, "He did not die alone. Nor would I say that you were not there when he needed you most, for you were there. Your love was always in his heart. And beyond that reality, every need was met by his Lord who was with him."

I realized that night how much more deeply than I had previously considered, we all yearn to know that death which struts before us all as the final separator will not ultimately isolate us from all and everyone we have known and loved, not even for a second, not to mention for a while. I realized again how blessed as Christians we are to know that in the death experience itself, Christians are not left during or afterwards…alone.

Little did I realize that night how much more I myself would soon need the truth of this conviction. You see, the diagnosis of that aneurism of the aorta turned out to be inaccurate. After months of carefully limiting my activities, and finally consenting to proceed with the needed surgical repair, it was discovered that my previous scans had been misread. The aorta was fine. A high hernia had been inaccurately identified. But in making this discovery, another problem that was very real was discovered.

I was rightly diagnosed with a malignant, cancerous tumor in my left kidney. "The silent killer," the doctors called it. And after an initial surgery to remove the cancerous tumor was botched by the "denuding" (that is the medical term. I call it simply cutting) of bones in my throat by a careless anesthesiologist, and several more months of recovery, I was taken to surgery a second time during which the cancerous tumor and a portion of my kidney were successfully removed.

I cannot count the occasions during those months of uncertainty, surgery and recovery, the times that the one awareness that enabled me to cope with the whole ordeal, was this: "As a Christian, you are not alone, and no matter what the next moment holds, you will never be alone!"

But of course, there would be no comfort even in the fact that Christians do not die alone, if a still greater fact were not true: Christians not only do not die *alone,* they do not die *forsaken!*

The Christ who is with us, will also keep us! Note that in every case study, or story, that I have shared, every individual had to some degree a vision of heaven, their destination. Furthermore, they all said that Jesus had come or soon was coming again. And when Jesus came "to get them," to lead them as He led His disciples who obediently followed Him long ago as recorded in the New Testament, they said that He would do so not to abandon them to *nowhere,* but to escort them to the epitome of the heavenly *somewhere,* to the heaven of their vision, where they would be eternally with God the Father, with Him and other loved ones.

Ultimate hope! From my perspective such hope is every person's heart's most ultimate need and desire.

I do not know if I ever asked her name. Her story and her

words are indelibly etched deeply within the pages of my memory. Over the years, as now in the writing of this book, they keep coming back to the forefront.

I met her only on this one occasion. The experience lasted no more than an hour. I was leaving the local hospital when, having completed my afternoon visits and exiting the front door, I saw her.

She was standing at the foot of the numerous steps that descended toward the parking lot, toward the left of the walkway facing the well-manicured shrubbery. She seemed as if she was hoping not to be seen, although she captured my gaze immediately.

She was young, surely not over thirty-five years of age, very slim, and petite. She was dressed in a sweatshirt, the logo I do not recall, and jeans somewhat disheveled. She appeared as if she had gotten dressed and hurried to the hospital without time to brush her hair or apply makeup.

But what provoked my gaze was her uncontrolled, unmuffled weeping. The sound of her cries reeked with pain. Her body seemed to convulse with every attempt to catch another breath. It was obvious that something was dreadfully wrong.

As I observed for a moment, I was reminded of the Biblical New Testament story of the Good Samaritan in which a man was beaten and injured by thieves, and was avoided by others who saw his situation but refused to get involved in lending him assistance(see Luke 10:25-37). No less than four or five other visitors to the hospital side-stepped her to ascend the steps into the hospital without even a word, extending only ominous, almost disapproving gazes.

The pastor's heart within me took over. I descended the steps, turned to her as she was still facing the shrubbery and said, "Lady, could you use a friend?" As she turned and looked towards me, I said, "My name is Logan Smith. I am the pastor of the local First Baptist Church. I hear and see your grief. I am willing to help you in any way that I can. Again, could you use a friend?"

She immediately began to tell me her story. She said, "I was in the house preparing to do the laundry when I heard the screams coming from outside the house. Running out the back door, I saw that the small barn not far from the house was on fire. Everything else becomes a blur...searching for my children who were outside somewhere playing, neighbors and people running up to see what was happening, fire trucks and an ambulance from out of nowhere, and a policeman.

"The first thing I remember clearly is the policeman. Asking me my name, he said, 'Come with me!' I said that I must find my children, and he responded, 'all your children have been located, but one of your sons has received burns and has been taken to the hospital. Come with me!'

"He brought me here while on the way explaining that my son and a neighbor's child had found a butane lighter and were playing with it. They went into the barn and decided to build a fire. Some gasoline stored there ignited. Both boys were burned.

"I still had no idea how badly my son was injured until I arrived. He was in an emergency treatment room being treated by a whole team of people for third degrees burns. I and the other mother had to wait in a private waiting room. We could not even be with them.

"My son was only eight years old. About an hour ago..." The

mother was not able to complete her sentence without falling up against me while weeping profusely. I simply extended that level of pastoral care that allows another simply to weep. But after a short while, she was able to compose herself enough to finish her sentence, "He died…He died.

"You said you are a pastor? Tell me something, please! Is there really a heaven? Did my son go there?

I remember distinctly saying to her, "Yes. I am so certain there is a heaven that I have, and will, put my own life and soul, on the line for it. Did your eight-year-old son go there? I will say that I have two grand reasons why I believe he did.

"For one thing, long ago a man named Abraham was having a heavy conversation with God. Abraham was pleading for the lives of others, specifically including many people who had been living very wickedly against God. Amid Abraham's pleading, he asked that question we have all asked which lies at the heart of what you are asking me. Abraham asked, 'Will the God of the heavens the judge of all the earth, do what is right?' The answer from heaven (Genesis 19:22ff personal translation) was, 'Yes! The God of the heavens, the judge of all the earth, will do what is right!'

"In regard to your son be assured, God will do what is right!

"But greater still for me is this fact: Jesus had and has a very special place for some people. For example, people who are impaired mentally do not need to fear. He has always made it clear that He would take care of them. But nobody, nobody did Jesus love more than the children! And he loves them still. Even when His own disciples became exhausted by the children and attempted to send them back home, He said, 'No! No! Always bring the children to me! For the very Kingdom of Heaven belongs to them!' (Matthew 19:13-14 personal translation).

"We do not have to worry about our young children as far as God doing what is right. We do not have to worry about God loving our children. God who we know in Jesus Christ loves them as we do and even greater still."

She then grabbed my arm as tightly as only a mother's desperation can and said, "Really? Really? Will you come with me and tell my whole family this? They all need to hear it! Then tell us all how to get to heaven where my son is. Will you do that please? Please?"

Her eyes revealed that what I had said had touched the very depth of her soul. I said, "Of course! Where is your family?"

She said, "They are still together in a room where a man who we were told was a hospital chaplain took us all. But he has said nothing to give us hope."

I asked, "What do you mean that a chaplain did not help you?"

She explained, "He said he was a volunteer, but I am not sure he should be allowed to talk to anybody." Her anger was extreme. This chaplain had no doubt only added to her grief. Soon I would understand. She added, "I asked him the same questions I asked you, 'Is heaven real? Did my son go there?'

"He said, 'Yes, heaven is real.' But then he said, 'Hell is too.' He went on to say 'If your son was eight years old, he was old enough to know whether he would make Jesus Lord of his life or not. If he had accepted Jesus as Lord and Savior of his life, he went to heaven. If he had not, he did not.'

"I screamed, 'You are saying that my eight-year-old boy went to hell?' He repeated, 'If your son had not accepted Jesus Christ as Lord and Savior of his life, he did not go to heaven.' Then I ran away. I ran all the way here.

"It was as if he wanted me to hear my dying son screaming again. Mister, I am not even sure what it means to accept Jesus Christ as Lord and Savior. I don't know that my family does either."

As I continued to walk with her to the room where her family was gathered, I must confess, I was having thoughts that were anything but pastoral toward a volunteer chaplain. I think I might have given him my best right cross against his chin and rearranged his appearance had I bumped into him. I surely might have been arrested for aggravated assault if upon confronting him he had arrogantly given me the same response to her questions.

Although I do not doubt that God may reveal Himself to some children at an early age, I could not imagine passing such an eternal, damning judgment on an eight year old little boy who had obviously not had the advantage of a Christian home. So, I remember repeating to her before we entered the room, "Remember God loves your son very, very much. He holds the ultimate power over all of us, and He will do what is right!"

The scene upon entering the room was as she had described. God surely was protecting me. The volunteer chaplain had obviously been quick to leave. He was nowhere to be seen or heard. There were about a dozen others in the room, all with swollen eyes and faces drenched in tears. Some individuals were holding others. Some sat alone…desperately alone.

She said with what they surely heard as a strange enthusiasm, given she had not long ago fled the room in desperation and unbridled grief, "Listen! I have some wonderful news! Listen!" As I reflect, it must have been something for her like resurrection morning was to Mary after having encountered Jesus alive. "Hear this!" she said.

I shared with them what I had shared with her. "God loves your child. God loves all the children. God loves you! And God who has ultimate authority and power will do what is right!"

The whole family seemed to immediately take a deep breath and to look up. One of them asked, "But what about us? Was the hospital chaplain correct?" But before I responded that person answered his own questions saying, "In case the chaplain was right about people who are really old enough to know who are no longer children, will you tell us what it means to accept Jesus Christ as Lord and Savior that we will know that we, too, will one day go to heaven and be where our child is?"

I did share the gospel with them. I shared the same Roman Road explanation that I related in the previous chapter. Then we all prayed together. I know of no one in that room who will not one day be with that child again in heaven.

But no one ever said it more succinctly than that grieving mother, "We all need the eternal hope that only a loving God can give."

All the stories recorded in this book affirm the truth. We have such a hope. No Christian dies alone. No Christian dies forsaken.

But does Holy Scripture back up these conclusions? Indeed, it does! Next chapter.

Chapter 10

The Affirmation of the Old Testament

Do the Holy Scriptures affirm the conclusions that no Christian dies alone or forsaken? Having asserted that they do and preparing to give examples to justify that position, I cannot assume that every reader of this book knows without my stating it what I mean by "Holy Scriptures." Various religions and religious sects across the globe, some of which are labeled as Christian, often claim their own collection of sacred scriptures.

Furthermore, in some countries within which I have had the privilege to visit and study, I have become aware that the word "Christian" is often used as a label to merely signify that a person is not Jewish or perhaps Muslim. In these cultures, likewise, to confess that I am a Christian and to refer to sacred Scripture may not necessarily communicate clearly which literary sources I have in mind.

My references to the Holy Scriptures are all rooted in my unwavering belief that The Holy Bible is the special written revelation of God of Himself in salvation history to us. By The Holy

Bible I refer to the thirty-nine books of the Old Testament and the twenty-seven books of the New Testament that comprise what is called "The Holy Cannon."

As valuable for historical and other study as they may be, I do not include the Apocryphal or Pseudepigraphal books, some of which were once widely published and sandwiched between the Old and New Testaments and can still be found in some translations or purchased at any bookstore.

The collection of sixty-six books historically known as the "The Holy Cannon," known most commonly as The Holy Bible is for me sacred scripture.

Does the Old Testament lend credibility to my conclusions as a Christian? After all, the Old Testament is undisputedly Hebrew literature. It is in its entirety a faith document, thoroughly Jewish.

I mean absolutely no criticism, ill-will or ill-thinking toward my Jewish friends, brothers, or sisters in asking this question: Does the Old Testament lend credibility to my conclusions as a Christian?

I am simply remembering an old Jewish Rabbi I had the privilege of meeting and under whose tutelage years ago I was privileged to study.

The year was 1980. The place was Jerusalem, Israel; or more specifically, "Tantur." Tantur in Hebrew means "hill." Although Jerusalem is geographically situated on seven hills, just outside the city, two-and-one-half miles from downtown, halfway to the neighboring city of Bethlehem, is a high hill just off the main highway. If you cited Tantur in Jerusalem in 1980, this site would immediately be the place that would be understood to be your meaning.

At first glance, this hill appeared very much to be the same as the others nearby. The hillside was peppered with olive trees tended by a residing shepherd and his sheep. But atop the hill amid the olive trees was a beautiful, small campus of buildings constructed out of the local Jerusalem stone.

The campus not only housed a monastery, but an educational institution that offered certain exclusive theological courses. Its official name was "The Tantur Ecumenical Institute for Advanced Theological Study." I use the word "exclusive" because at that time, still in its early beginnings, one could study at Tantur certain curricula only at their invitation; however, today I understand Tantur is open to anyone, no longer exclusive.

So it was a great, humbling privilege for me to be invited by Dr. Wayne Ward of The Southern Baptist Theological Seminary, where I was a student, along with twelve others from the greater United States, to travel to Tantur and study while, in so doing, earning a semester of credit hours.

Tantur had an inhouse theologian, Dr. Brown, from California, whose official title I do not recall. Dr. Brown had structured our course of study as an inquiry into "Our Biblical Roots." The faculty of Tantur coordinated many of the classroom lectures to include visiting faculty from the Hebrew University of Jerusalem, which, along with the Vatican and Notre Dame University, had brought Tantur into existence.

That was the setting within which I met a most distinguished gentleman. We all knew him simply as Rabbi Peli. We were told that not only was he highly influential within the academic world, but he was extremely influential in the political world. He was the department head at the Hebrew University in Jerusalem of the study of Hebrew history, specifically the Hebraic sacrificial system, including its feasts and celebrations, but he was also a best friend and personal political advisor to the Prime Minister of Israel.

But from the moment we met, and I am certain all the others participating in the study would avow the same, we were not merely faculty and students or diplomat and foreign allies. We were colleagues. We were friends. It was obvious that this was the relationship Rabbi Peli desired. Rather than be called "Dr. Peli," he preferred simply with a smile and an outstretched hand of kindness, "Just call me Rabbi."

Rabbi Peli was the epitome of the stereotype. He was short, stout, and round. He had the physical appearance of Santa Claus, but dressed in distinguished black. Although he had the typical beard, I really do not know how his prayer cap stayed so well in place on his balding head. But it did.

But the two most strikingly things about him were his intellect and his smile. He had a brilliant mind. He knew his field of study, and he knew it well. Further, he was most gifted in his ability to share it. His smile was infectious as he took great joy in sharing the history of his Orthodox Jewish faith, which he acknowledged was also the history of our Christian faith.

But his joy was more than simply rooted in his field of study and faith. It was rooted in people. As the days passed, one could see it reflected in his growing relationship with us all. For although each day his last lecture of the evening with us would often not end until ten p.m. or later, he would routinely remain and just chat with us. As my classmates did, I learned to love Rabbi Peli. I thanked our Lord for him. I still do.

But that last evening we all spent with him in the classroom is an occasion I remember with a heavy heart, precisely because of that affection. The last lecture had been formally concluded. Rabbi Peli who was seated at the head table from where he had taught us, said, "Rarely, have I done this. But I feel and believe that our relationship which I will miss affords us the opportunity.

"As my Christian friends, I have observed your keen and sincere interest in understanding rightly the Jewish faith. For this reason, I want to extend to you the opportunity to ask me any question regarding any area of the Jewish faith you wish. I will be forthright and give you my best answer to whatever you ask."

We understood that what the rabbi was extending to us was an act of sheer kindness, scholastic respect, trust, and friendship. We understood that it was a rare opportunity indeed.

Molly Marshall, a fellow student and friend, more widely known today as Dr. Molly Marshall-Green, a theological scholar and educator, was seated to my left. The late Dr. John Claypool, a former pastor, scholar, author, and friend was seated to my right. We all took a moment to exchange gazes with one another as if to ask, "Which of us will ask the first question?"

Molly was the first among us all to seize the opportunity. Her question was the one that has for me forever defined that moment. She asked, "My question is an eschatological one. As Christians, we are familiar with the Jewish concept of Sheol, the gloomy place of all the dead. We are aware of the Jewish belief that immortality is achieved through the lineage of one's children. We are aware that the Jewish faith looks also for immortality through the physical, literal rebuilding of the Temple in Jerusalem.

"But Rabbi, apart from Sheol, from the continuation of your

family tree, from the rebuilding of the physical Temple in Jerusalem, which we all may or may not live long enough on this earth to see, what hope within the Jewish faith do you have for a life beyond death in any form of Heavenly existence?"

One would have had to be blind, deaf, and totally oblivious to the question and the moment not to have noticed the instantaneous change that occurred within the atmosphere of that classroom and most poignantly the person of Rabbi Peli. Suddenly, for the first time in all the weeks we had spent with him, his countenance totally changed.

The sparkle in his eye disappeared. His straight-forward gaze turned downward. His impeccable posture was transformed as his shoulders seemed to slump. His voice lowered in tenor and volume. This hopeful man seemed suddenly changed, as though he was staring into a dark abyss, looking for anything to hold onto, but seeing nothing. The only three words he gave in response to the question were, "We have none."

The moments of silence following his statement seemed like an eternity, until finally someone asked, "But, Rabbi, what about the various references in the Old Testament regarding 'abiding in the House of the Lord forever?'(see Psalm 23)."

In my mind I am still trying to peel back the layers of meaning within his response. Said he, "Remembering the original question and its acknowledgement of the rebuilding of the Temple, the House of God, in Jerusalem, never confuse the Jewish concept of the House of God and the Christian view of heaven."

For all practical purposes, our time with Rabbi Peli was over. I do not recall any further questions that evening, although I am certain others were asked. I recall only expressions of gratitude for the experience and farewell wishes. But I remember his words of response to the question of the Jewish perspective of life after death as if it were yesterday: "We have none."

Now I realize that the Rabbi was speaking from a very conservative, purely orthodox point of view. After decades of study and reflection on the subject, I have come to realize that there are distinctly different views of life beyond death in other branches of Judaism.

For instance, some later Jewish schools of thought advocate a strong belief in life beyond death, citing foremost the book of Job 19:25-27, the book of Isaiah 26:19, and the book of Daniel 12:1-3.

Still other Jewish schools of thought cite Psalm 9, Psalm 16, Psalm 23, Psalm 49, Psalm 73, I Samuel 28, and II King 2, along with other varied, but limited texts.

Adding to the complexity of their interpretation of these texts in regard to the subject of eschatology are questions that include: (1) Does God taking a mortal away to an immortal realm for an unspecified amount of time constitute death being eternally transcended by life? (2) Given the various types of death in Jewish thought, including the death of desire, of bareness, of famine, of grief, do these texts refer to a resurrected eternal life? (3) Why does the idea of life beyond death in the Hebrew texts seem to appear only in the latter prophetic literature? Other questions are many.

I have no answers for these questions. I cannot claim to fully fathom even their inquiry. If I could, to do so is a task for another time, place, and writing.

I only mention such things to reaffirm that within the Jewish faith there is no clear or universally accepted belief regarding life after death, or more specifically, eternal life in heaven even when the views of the Talmud and the Mishnah are included with the Old Testament in the Jewish collection of sacred scriptures.

But the rabbi's point of concern-- "Do not confuse the Jewish concept of the House of God and the Christian view of life after death in heaven,"--is well taken. For in this he is right. When he read the Old Testament, he was reading with a "forward" gaze. He was looking forward yet to the coming of the Messiah and the fulfillment of Old Testament prophecy.

But as Christians, as a rule, we do not read the Old Testament so much with a "forward" gaze as we do with an "historical" gaze. Christians believe the Messiah has come, and the Old Testament prophecy has been and is fulfilled in Him. Christians acknowledge this belief in His name, Jesus Christ, meaning "Jesus the Messiah." That is why Christians read the Old Testament with a focused gaze, not as the Rabbi who reads the Old Testament with a forward gaze; meaning, focused upon our past to more fully understand our present and future.

That fact was reinforced to me several years later when I returned to Israel, not to study at Tantur, but at the request of Dr. Wayne Ward to deliver evening lectures amid a two-week tour of the Holy Land to some one hundred and fifty participants. My responsibility was to explain the significance of the sites they were to visit the following day. This tour and lectures were inclusive of sites in both the countries of Israel and Jordan and were of Old Testament and New Testament significance.

We were spending one of several nights in Jerusalem. One memorable evening, for reasons I do not recall, my spirit was restless. I could not sleep. So, I did something that many people might find strange. Remembering both from years before how deeply moved I had been visiting the "Western Wall," known perhaps more widely as "the wailing wall," and Dr. Brown of Tantur having said, "If you ever want to visit the real Western Wall, do so in the black of night in the wee hours of the morning," I did exactly that.

It was about two a.m. when I walked outside the front door of the Ambassador Hotel. I began walking toward the old city where the Western Wall is located. Hardly had I began walking along the sidewalk when a "me'nigt" or taxi, appeared. Pulling alongside the curb, the driver asked if I would like to ride.

I asked, "How much to travel to the Western Wall?" to which he responded, "mon'eh," meaning "meter." Being aware that it was neither the Sabbath nor an airport destination, hence no surcharge was required, and no use of the meter was legally mandated, I said, "No," and I made him a counter offer, in Israeli money, of course.

As was the custom, the bartering began. It ended as I walked away saying, "No, thank you," at which point the driver smiled and accepted my final offer. He did ask, "Why go to the Western Wall at this hour?" I explained my curiosity citing what Dr. Brown had said and my inability to sleep to which he said most interestingly, "That is one of the places we locals go when we are looking for answers, too."

In only a few minutes we were there, whereupon I bartered for a ride back to the hotel within forty-five minutes to an hour. It did not take long for me to realize that Dr. Brown was right. One visiting Israel, especially a Christian, needs to go to the Western Wall in the wee hours of the morning amid the darkness to get the "real" story of the wall.

History books rightly tell us that the Western Wall was constructed beginning sometime around 40 BC by Herod the Great. But he did not live to complete it. Construction of the wall continued even after his death. The section of the wall visible today is just a small segment of a more far-reaching retaining wall which was part of the encasement of the hilltop that allowed for the expansion and support of the huge flat paved area known today as "the temple mount."

Atop this flat area was the ever-expanding great second Jewish Temple, inclusive of the Holy of Holies, which stood until leveled by the Roman army under Titus in 70 A.D., just as Jesus had foretold.

The Western Wall, although not technically a part of the Temple's specific structure, is held in great reference by the Jewish people because it did support the temple; and moreover still, because this section of the Western Wall stands close to where the Holy of Holies stood, the Holy of Holies being within the temple where the Jews believed God Himself lived.

Given that this flat area where the temple stood is not under Jewish control today, the Jews acknowledge the site of the Western Wall to be their Holy place for unsurpassed intimacy with God. I write this, intending in no degree to slight the sacredness to the Jewish faith of the synagogue or other sacred sites used in their worship.

Of course, the Western Wall has been a site surrounded by some misunderstanding which many Jews and others find offensive. That is, the term "wailing wall" is not an historical or accurate description of the worship that occurs there. Proponents of the term have advocated it is justified because the Jewish people who go there to worship are weeping and wailing over the fallen Temple which is no more.

But even if a casual tourist is only slightly observant, he or she will quickly discern that although a worshipper may shed a tear, the movements and sounds of those involved are not those of distraught individuals uncontrollably weeping, wailing or grieving over something that once existed long ago.

Rather, the movements of the worshippers, particularly those of the young men of the Hasidic sect of orthodox Judaism that one will see on any given day swaying backward and forward, are rhythmically coordinated with the words, not being wailed, but being intoned. You see, the people too often stereotyped as weeping and wailing are in fact chanting and praying.

And their prayers being chanted are not random thoughts. By and large, they are prayers from the Siddur, the Jewish prayer book. So, it is easy to comprehend why some Jews are offended by the term, "wailing wall." They are before the wall in sincere, traditional prayer and worship. They are not wailing. That is what one sees when they visit the wall as hundreds, even thousands, of people do every day.

But what a striking difference it was to visit the Western Wall during the late hour and black of night. As Dr. Brown had said, that is when I saw "the" Western Wall and learned of the tradition and worship that the general public rarely sees or hears.

The wall was lighted, but somewhat dimly. It certainly lacked the scintillating brilliance of the sunlight reflecting off the Jerusalem limestone.

There were no crowds. The plaza was empty. There were no young men of the Hasidim praying, chanting, and acting out their worship in front of the wall. In total, on this night there were less than a dozen other people at this most Holy place. All were very elderly men who, identifiable by their dress, were very devout Orthodox leaders within the Jewish faith. Perhaps they were all rabbis, but I did not ask.

I was approached by one of the men who said, "It is most unusual to have anyone come to the wall at this hour, much less a person who is not of the Jewish faith."

I have since concluded that he surmised that I was not Jewish because I was not wearing a prayer cap, a "yarmulke." He asked, "Why are you here?"

Sensing the sincere, non-threatening interest in his voice, I responded, "I am here to learn. I am a Christian, but I deeply desire to more fully understand my faith by more deeply understanding the Jewish faith in which it has its roots. When I say to someone that I am a Judeo-Christian, I want to be able to explain what that truly means."

Before he could respond, I mentioned that in the past I had been a student of Rabbi Peli's and that he and I had become friends. "I know the Rabbi well," he said with a smile. "A friend of his is a friend of mine."

I returned his smile and an outstretched hand. After a few minutes I asked, "I am surprised, frankly, to have found anyone at the wall at this hour. Tell me, is this a common practice?"

He smiled and with a slight nod of his head said, "Yes. But as you see, when the crowds of tourist retire for the day, everyone except for a few of us older men do likewise. Some of our group remain here. Others of our group retire for the evening. We routinely divide the days of the week and the hours of the night among us so that the wall is never unattended, and the prayers never cease. At least one of us will be at the wall, praying, chanting our prayers every hour of the day and night. The prayers must never cease."

I was amazed that night as the old man spoke those words to me. I am no less moved as I remember them and record them on this page. I am moved by men and women so devoted to prayer. I only can wish that Christians I know were as committed to the importance and possibilities of prayer.

I then asked him, "But tell me, please, I understand the chanting of the prayers. Rabbi Peli gave me a copy of the Siddur, which I cherish and read to this day. But what is the meaning of the bodily movements, the swaying of the upper body forward and backward, while one is chanting the prayers? Why are the movements sometimes rapid and exaggerated, while at other times they seem much more intentional and subdued? I notice that the older men are now making the same movements as the younger men that I have observed during the day, however the movements of the older men seem to be much more measured. The older men are moving much more slowly, even gravely."

He hesitated for a moment as if to organize his words, and I think, decide if he would even share them. Then he said, "You are most observant to notice this. Given the hour, you are no doubt sincere in your desire to understand. Therefore, I will explain. If you come during the day when the young men are praying, and demonstrably augmenting their prayers with their bodily movements and you ask them, 'Why?' they will not tell you that they are really trying to impress you, which without a doubt some of them are.

"They will tell you that they are imitating the movements of our forefathers as they left Egypt and came to the promised land of Israel, riding on the backs of their camels and burros. If you have ever ridden a camel any distance, for logical reasons you will move in cadence with their walk, swaying backwards and forwards. So, they will tell you that they are trying in every way to pray as the Fathers of our Faith have always prayed out of gratitude, tradition, and the peace of the prayer itself."

Then I said, "But, if I am hearing you correctly, that is not really what is at the root of the meaning of the movement, is it?"

I saw it happen again, just as I had seen it years ago in the person of Rabbi Peli. The countenance of this old man, a Jewish leader, fell. His voice deepened and his gaze seemed to drift far off as he said, "No…No…and that's why you see the difference in our movements as we pray. The truth is, we are making those movements as we all pray in a simple, but dire effort to *get God's attention!*

"We have not heard from God for a long time. We keep praying, and pleading through our gestures, that just maybe, even tonight, God will break the hundreds of years of silence and speak to us again. Maybe He will send us the Messiah for whom we have waited for so long."

His words were not only heavy upon his lips, but equally weighed heavily upon my mind and heart. For no sooner had he spoken them, that I looked up and gazed back toward the face of the wall. What did I see?

In one specific line of sight, I saw what to me told the story of salvation history while contrasting my Christian faith with the Jewish faith, through which it all became revealed.

For immediately above the top of the wall, I saw the golden dome of the Mosque of Omar, known also as the Dome of the Rock, which sits on the exact site of the great Jewish temple inclusive of the Holy of Holies. Having been inside the Mosque, I remembered that directly underneath the dome is the great rock of sacrifice upon which immeasurable amounts of blood was spilled by individuals seeking through their sacrifices a restored ideal relationship with God as it was in the Edenic beginning.

In my mind I could see the men and women of centuries past doing exactly what these older men before the wall were desperately doing; trying to get God's favorable attention while looking for the possible coming of the Messiah, and working without reservation for salvation.

But then above the top of the Dome of the Mosque of Omar, the site of the Holy of Holies, it occurred to me that I was also seeing the darkened outline of the Mount of Olives, the very last place where Jesus stood following his resurrection before his ascension into heaven and the place where it is believed that He will return upon his second coming.

Perceiving Christ atop the Mount of Olives, it was reaffirmed in my spirit that He was the Messiah for whom the Jewish people had long awaited and prayed. His shed blood from the cross on Calvary for the forgiveness of sins and redemption of all men and women who would accept its efficacy and believe in Him had accomplished what all the centuries of spilled blood within the Temple below could not. And, yes, He will come again, but next time not primarily to redeem, but rather to gather His people while pronouncing judgment on the remainder of the world.

That was my vision: the older men standing, desperately

pleading in prayer to get the Lord's attention, in the shadow beneath the Holy of Holies, beneath the shadow of the Mount of Olives, beneath the reality of the Living Lord who is the Messiah who has already come.

Although I knew that this older Jewish man to whom I was speaking, as well as the others at the wall, saw the same images and understood the tenants of the Christian faith as did I, I still wanted to literally cry out to him, "My brother, don't you see? Will you not see? You do not have to desperately seek God's love and attention. You already have it. You do not have to look for the Messiah to come. In Jesus Christ He has already come. You are praying beneath his veritable shadow. You do not have to seek hope, rather through Him, hope is seeking you."

Nevertheless, as we continued to share, I knew that when I left it would be again like it was when I last said goodbye to my friend Rabbi Peli. I would leave and return to the Ambassador Hotel with the eternal hope in Jesus Christ within my heart and soul. He and his brothers at the wall would continue with "no hope beyond this world" as the rabbi had stated it. They would continue to chant and pray in their quest to get God's attention. My hope for them all still rests in the awareness that when the great day of eternal accounting comes, God will be true to Himself, leaving no man or woman a justifiable excuse for not loving Him, obeying Him, and trusting Him, and He will do what is right.

But the experience of that night reaffirmed what Rabbi Peli said about the Hebrew scriptures. As a member of the Jewish faith, a Jew reads the Old Testament scriptures with a "forward" gaze, while a Christian, as a believer and follower of Jesus Christ, reads the Old Testament scriptures with a historically "focused" gaze. Christians cannot read the Old Testament scriptures without bringing to them an awareness of what Jesus did, what Jesus says, and that which Jesus yet promises to do. Again, Christians believe that all truth and revelation, including the Hebrew scriptures, find their fulfillment in Him.

So, I repeat my previous question, acknowledging that my reading of the Hebrew scriptures is predicated upon my Christian faith and perspective: "Do the Hebrew scriptures, the Old Testament, support my conclusions based on the case studies presented in this book that no Christian dies alone and no Christian dies forsaken?"

Yes, I believe Old Testament scripture does. I believe Job, Daniel and Isaiah do speak to the subjects as do certain other texts.

Job could well have been describing an occasion such as "the visitation" experiences I have described in the previous chapters when he said, "For I know that my Redeemer lives, and at last He will stand upon the earth, and after my skin has been thus destroyed, then from my flesh I shall see God whom I shall see at my side, and my eyes shall behold (Him), and not another." (Job 19:25-27a, RSV).

Daniel's words sound very similar to those of the Apostle Paul speaking to the church in Thessalonica when he said, regarding God's people never being forsaken, "At that time shall arise Michael, the great prince who has charge of your people. And there shall be a time of trouble, such as never has been since there was a nation till that time; but at that time your people shall be delivered, everyone whose name shall be found written in the book. And many of those who sleep in the dust of the earth shall awake, some to everlasting life, and some to shame and everlasting contempt …" (Daniel 12:1-2 RSV).

Isaiah puts it most succinctly, "The dead shall live, their bodies shall rise" (Isaiah 27:19a RSV).

But of all the texts in the Hebrew scriptures that seem to go hand in hand with the experiences of the process of dying I have shared in this book, is that most beloved, in my opinion, of all texts by people of all ages and eras. It was one of the first passages of scripture I learned to quote from memory as a child. I write of Psalm 23.

The initial verse of the Psalm is the bedrock of the entire Psalm. Every word of hope and praise in the Psalm finds its basis in this, "The Lord is my Shepherd I shall not want ..." (1:1 RSV).

Interestingly, this fact was brought home to me by my late friend and brother Dr. Solomon Abegunde. Solomon and I were classmates at The Southern Baptist Theological Seminary in Louisville, Kentucky. That cold, snowy January day in 1978, when we first met, we became joined not only in the quest to learn, but at the heart. I believe I know exactly what King David felt toward Jonathan. I loved Solomon Abegunde and his family. Solomon loved me and my family.

Until his grave illness and subsequent death, no matter where he was in the world, including his home country of Nigeria, not a week went by that we did not somehow speak with one another and pray together.

Solomon studied linguistics. His calling from the beginning of his public ministry was to translate the whole of the Bible into the language of the Yoruba, his native tribe. Solomon had begun the task with a friend who was serving as the President of the Baptist Seminary in Legos at the same time Solomon was Pastor of the First Baptist Church of Legos. But the president of the Seminary had been killed in a tragic automobile accident shortly after the task was begun, leaving Solomon, lacking the linguistic skills for such a project, alone to complete the translation.

Solomon resigned his pastorate. He left his wife, Deborah, and six children in Nigeria to come to The Southern Baptist Theological Seminary to receive the training to complete the task, thinking at the time that he would not see his family again for at least two to three years.

On the day we first met, I remarked that I did not know if I could have made such a sacrifice, whereupon he took me to his room and showed me no less than a dozen wood figures. They were faces carved in an ebony wood. Noting that one of them caught my attention, he took it off the shelf above his desk and said, "Take it. As you seek to fulfill God's call in your life, if you are ever tempted to quit or stop short, look at it and remember. Then return to your work and be faithful."

He explained, "That is what I have to do. If I did not look at these every day, I might be more than tempted to quit, go home, and leave the translation of the Bible into Yoruba to someone else. You see, each of these carvings is an idol. Each belonged to a member of my birth family. The idols were carved and empowered by the tribal witch doctor. The one I am giving you belonged to one of my grandmothers.

"She, like the others of my family, sometimes went hungry because what little she had she believed had to be offered as a burnt offering to her idol. She and my family did not have the Scriptures. They still do not. It hurts me to think of this, but the pain is not without some meaning. I cannot quit. I must open the Scriptures for all of my family and my people."

I cannot tell you how many times over the years I have been hurt, exhausted or despondent and felt like quitting. But upon those occasions I have looked at that wooden figure which to this day still sits above my desk. I have remembered Solomon's words of love, encouragement, and wisdom. And having done so, I have refocused with a renewed resolve. No, Solomon did not quit. Though I miss him, neither can I.

Solomon did graduate with honors in the field of linguistics. He was immediately hired by the International Bible Society, from which he ultimately retired before becoming President of a second seminary in the state of Oyo, Nigeria, and eventually, due to illness, living out his last years in the United States. He did complete the first translation of the Bible into Yoruba. In addition, he contributed to over thirty other translations. His work continues to be a major contribution to linguistics and the spread of the Christian gospel.

It was he who said to me one day as we were spending time together in Cornelia, Georgia, and discussing the twenty-third Psalm, "Of all the texts I have been asked to translate, none has proven to be more challenging than Psalm 23:1, 'The Lord is my shepherd I shall not want.' (RSV).

"The challenge has not been to rightly translate the words, 'The Lord,'" said he, "Rather, the problem has been that one word 'shepherd.' The word 'shepherd,' is among many cultures of the world, a most respectable term, but in an equal number of other cultures it is not. For example, in my own tribe of the Yoruba, a shepherd is not considered to be someone to be respected, loved, praised, or much less worshipped. The shepherd is not thought to be a person who merely cares for animals.

"Rather, the word 'shepherd' suggests the image of a highwayman, a thief. At its best, the term suggests a chiseler, what you might call a 'con-man' or a nomadic gypsy looking for his next victim.

"So, the challenge I faced with other translators was how to translate the term 'shepherd' to all who might read the text conveying the Psalmist's true intent. After many hours of discussion with colleagues who faced the same dilemma and much prayer asking for divine guidance, I translated the verse this way: "The Lord is the one who is all I need."

To this day, acknowledging the most meaningful images and realities I have experienced of Christ as the gospel shepherd, and how deeply I cherish those New Testament texts that reveal Christ as the loving care-giving Shepherd of all of us who follow Him, I must confess that Solomon's translation enables me to even more fully grasp and appreciate the totality of Psalm 23.

It also raises this awareness: In that ultimate moment of drawing one's last physical breath on this earth, that is the question of questions, is it not? For in that single moment, a person's definitive answer is revealed to the question of questions: "To whom do you look for your hope of anything and everything?"

This is what I have heard every person I have cited in this book say. It is what without exception I have heard countless other Christians whose stories I have not told say. It is what now and in the moment of my own death I intend to continue to say: "The Lord is the one who is all I need!"

It is true, as the Psalmist says, in life. It is true in death. This is the underlying declaration I could hear every person I have cited avowing as they sang with the Psalmist, "Even though I walk through the valley of the shadow of death, I fear no evil, for thou art with me; thy rod and thy staff, they comfort me (23:4, RSV)... the Lord is the one who is all I need" or again in my words, "No Christian dies alone and no Christian dies forsaken."

It was a hot summer day in Israel when Dr. Brown of Tantur said to me and my classmates, "Today we are going on a long hike. We will need plenty of water and to rest along the way. But as challenging as it shall be, I believe you will find it worth it."

On all accounts Dr. Brown was right. We were taken by bus just outside the city of Jerusalem on the King's highway toward Jericho. It is fourteen miles from Jerusalem to Jericho, and I am to this day thankful that he did not require us to walk every mile of the way, even though it is all downhill. But not too far along the way, Dr. Brown said, "Now we walk."

I would learn later that this educational and inspirational walk is one that has been and is often undertaken by Christians visiting the Holy Land. It follows the old route depicted within the New Testament in various stories, especially that of the Good Samaritan, and the one believed by many scholars to have been in the mind of King David, perhaps, when he wrote Psalm 23.

The winding route is often cited as the Wadi Quelt. The old route winds up, down, and along the rocky, barren, high hillsides that afford little to no opportunities for short cuts or straying too far off the way.

But if one descends to the very nadir of the Wadi, as Dr. Brown noted that day, one gains a new appreciation for Psalm 23. For there is a very specific path along the route that Dr. Brown said had for centuries been known as "the valley of the shadow." It was so named because, being wedged between the cliffs that stand hundreds of feet tall to each side, even on the brightest of days, it was (and is) dark, extremely hot and foreboding. Worse still, the place was dangerous. This was the place where it was far too common for a traveler to be robbed, beaten, even killed. So eventually, the "valley of shadow" became known as "the valley of the shadow of death."

Did David have this place in mind? Of course, I do not know. But I still recall the "chill" that went down my spine invoked by this place, the ominous atmosphere it created. When I delved more deeply into Psalm 23 with my friend Solomon, he emphasized this too: When David spoke of the valley of the shadow of death, his choice and linkage of words suggests the most ominous, the greatest threats one can ever image to his or her existence.

So, I have reached this conclusion. Whatever geographical place David may have had in mind matters little, although my visit to this historical place was valuable and meaningful. For David in the use of the term valley of the shadow of death is really talking about that existential place in me and in you, in every person, where the greatest threats, fears and death itself lurk in the darkness of the unknown, awaiting their every opportunity to take from us what we cherish most.

To this David said, "I am not alone. The Lord is with me and He is all I need."

I personally like those words "with me." I like the way they are coupled with "As I walk through." I am deeply moved by, and find meaningful, the reaffirmation that there is life beyond death because I am walking through death, not into death to abide there, but through! I am not entering death with the idea that the Lord will meet me on the other side of death. Rather, the Psalmist says that He is with me every step of the way from here to there…as I, we, together, walk through it all.

As David, the Psalmist, put it, I cannot think of anyone I had rather have with me, or who could do for me that which only the Lord can. Remember how David put it, "Thy rod and thy staff they comfort me" (v.4b, RSV).

Were the rod and staff two separate instruments? In terms of David seeking to stress two realities, likely "yes." But were the rod and the staff in the hands of a literal shepherd two separate instruments? My thought is, "not likely." Rather, in the hands of the shepherd, both instruments, I believe, are incorporated into a long, but strong, slender pole with an elongated hook at the top akin to that of a fishhook without the barb.

Such a "shepherd's staff" would support both images. Consider "the rod." The Hebrew word is "sebet." It suggests a short weapon like a medieval mace which is used primarily as a protective weapon. Such a rod could be used as a mode of defense against an attacking enemy or beast. It could be deadly in that its blows were characteristically powerful.

However, there are some interpreters that say, within a royal setting, this rod is more of a scepter than a mace, less a weapon and more of a visible sign of the King's authority and power.

Personally, I have an idea that both meanings might well have been in the Psalmist's mind as he describes the Lord who walks with me through the valley of the shadow of death. For He, in so doing, is my protector and has both the authority and power to see to it that death cannot, will not, hurt or destroy me.

And the staff? The staff is sometimes called by shepherds, "my walking stick." At least this is what my shepherd friends at

Tantur, Israel, called it. The Hebrew word for staff is "mis'enet." A staff is much longer than a mere rod or scepter. Its additional length combined with the distinctive hook on the end makes it most useful as a tool for the shepherd for the purpose of guiding his sheep along the way as well as rescuing sheep who have strayed or fallen by "catching them with the hook" from dangerous situations or precarious circumstances.

So, the staff is a source of help in weakness, guidance in confusion, and encouragement in bewilderment. Combining the two instruments of the rod and the staff into the shepherd's staff affords through the hands of the one who wields it: power, protection, confidence, and direction.

Even a dumb and half-seeing sheep can confidently follow a shepherd who rightly wields such a rod and staff. Reading the Psalm while remembering the New Testament--that states that Jesus, the Good Shepherd, loves us all as His sheep--I cannot help but in joy sing along with David. "The Lord is the one who is all I need." Indeed, I can follow and walk along-side the Lord who has such wisdom, love, power, and authority. I can do so not only in life, but also through death, the passage to heavenly eternal life. His rod and His staff, even in the anticipation of death, as they do amid the process of death, comfort me.

And "the comfort" is, given the roles of the rod and staff, I need not fear or despair. For I am not now, nor shall I ever be, left alone to face anything, or forsaken when confronted by any threat.

That is what I heard repeatedly my friends saying as they punctuated their visitations and experiences of death, often with Jesus within their range of vision, with the simple words, "It's okay. Tell my family, my friends, everybody who will hear. It's okay."

David concludes Psalm 23 with a shout of praise, "And I shall dwell in the house of the Lord forever!" (23:6b RSV). I know that Rabbi Peli would say that the meaning of this statement is actually, "I will take refuge in the Temple where God is; God who is both good and merciful. As I abide in the temple my troubled life will be calmed and disordered life will be restructured whereby; I will no longer lose the awareness of His love and care as long as I live." That is how the Rabbi would interpret it.

But reading these words as a Christian, my interpretation is *eternally* different. I do hear again what my dying friends described, saying, "Heaven is real. Heaven is beautiful. He (the Lord) says that it is time for me to come there. I want to go with Him. I want to be with Him there."

I suppose every person whose story I have recorded in this book could have written the twenty-third Psalm.

So back to my original question, "Do the Hebrew scriptures, specifically the Old Testament, support the authenticity of the testimony of the Christians at the moment of their death presented in this book?"

"Yes!" For me they do. Psalm 23 specifically is almost a verbatim of the experiences of not only these to which I have alluded in the opening chapters, but numerous others which I have witnessed and heard over a lifetime of vocational ministry.

But the greater question still remains: "Though I walk through the valley of the shadow of death, I will fear no evil; for thou art with me; thy rod and thy staff, they comfort me…and I shall dwell in the House of the Lord forever" (Psalm 23:4,6b RSV). Did Jesus, Himself, believe such a thing?

Did Jesus Himself ever promise His disciples, including you

About the Author

Dr. Smith served as Pastor of local churches in the Southern United States for over forty years. He also served as an adjunct professor in Biblical studies and a staff writer for a Christian publication. He is a graduate of Mercer University and the Southern Baptist Theological Seminary in Louisville, Kentucky. He has also studied abroad at the Tantur Institute for Advanced Theological Study in Jerusalem, Israel.

and me, such a thing? It is one thing to hear David sing it. It is another thing to hear the Apostle Paul preach it. It is still another thing to hear Dr. Luke in his two-volume work, Luke-Acts, say it. And it is still another thing to hear Timothy, John, Peter, or any of the other New Testament writers declare it.

But did Jesus, Himself, promise as the Psalmist wrote, as my friends have testified, that as His followers we will not die alone or forsaken? After all, as a Christian believer, it is only His promise that ultimately matters. For in Him alone is life possible…now and forever!

Chapter 11

The Affirmation of the New Testament

The New Testament is our primary written revelation of who Jesus Christ was, the earthly life He lived, and the words He spoke. Most importantly, it is our primary revelation of who Jesus *is*. As I have stated previously, I am referring to the twenty-seven books of the New Testament proper. I do not include the New Testament Apocryphal (meaning "false") books or the New Testament Pseudepigraphal (meaning "hidden") books.

"Is the experience of death within the life of a Christian specifically addressed by Jesus?" Asking this question reminds me of an occasion that occurred within the classroom of the late Dr. Dale Moody of The Southern Baptist Theological Seminary in Louisville, Kentucky, where I was a student.

It occurred during the senior year of my Master of Divinity curricula. I had developed a deep respect for Dr. Moody who, admittedly among Baptist at the time, was a controversial figure. He was considered controversial particularly because of his views on historical premillennial eschatology and the perseverance of efficacious faith.

Dr. T. Logan Smith

I can only wish his critics could have known him and sat in his classes as I did. I was especially moved by the personal testimony of his salvation experience. He shared it at the beginning of each semester class. Without exception, he did so with great emotion, tears, gratitude, and praise for the Christ in whom he believed. He is the only professor I have witnessed, when sharing in the classroom, how he learned the scriptures so thoroughly, and he did, wipe his moist eyes saying, "No other such beautiful words have been written."

I could see him, as he described it, as a boy plowing behind a mule the long furrows of the vast field. I could envision him at the end of the furrow, taking his Bible out of the bib of his overalls, reading a verse before putting it away, and memorizing that verse by repeating it over and over again for the length of the furrow, where he would stop, reach into the bib of his overalls again for his Bible, and repeat the process.

That is how he emotionally told it with his great love for the Scriptures. That is how he virtually memorized the New Testament as a prelude to becoming a renowned theologian and Greek Scholar.

Regardless of what his critics said about him, he lived the faith he professed. According to another professor I deeply loved and respected, at no point was Dr. Moody's faith more apparent that at his own death. As he related it to me, Dr. Moody had developed blockages in his arteries. In those days, by-pass surgery was still in its infancy.

The year was 1992. He was scheduled for the dangerous surgery. He was awaiting transfer to the operating room when the physician came into his hospital room and said, "I am facing a dilemma. You need this by-pass, but I have another patient who I believe will not live until tomorrow without immediate surgery. Dale, I do believe that your condition will allow us to delay your surgery for a few days to allow me to treat the other patient. But only you know exactly what difficulty you are experiencing. I foremost respect that fact. So, tell me precisely how you are feeling so that we can decide what is best for you."

Dr. Moody, being the man of God I knew him to be, really would not have the discussion. Rather, I am told that he emphatically said, "Perform the surgery on the other patient. I will give him my slot in the operating room. I will delay and simply trust the Lord's judgment in the matter. I believe it is what Jesus would do."

Some days later, Dr. Moody's surgery was rescheduled. It was with a grieving heart that another theologian and relative of Dr. Moody shared with me that Dr. Moody had his visitation and died in the elevator on the way to surgery. He literally gave his life for another. But greater still, through obedience to his calling, he gave his life for all of us. Yes, I believe that he was right. That is what Jesus would have done…that is in fact, what Jesus did.

I wish all his critics could have known this man who, though labeled a heretic by some, loved the Lord, and loved the scriptures.

But the class I recall that prompted me telling his story occurred in 1980. The theology course was focused on "The New Testament and The Holy Spirit." It was early in the semester when Dr. Moody addressed the subject of the Holy Spirit as our shield against all evil and its manifestations, including evil, unholy spirits.

I do not remember the exact specifics of the young student's objection to Dr. Moody's presentation. I do remember that he was a "young" student, because others of us who had a bit more experience as students in seminary had at least by our junior year learned three things: (1) We knew that we did not have all the answers. (2) We knew that any belief that could be challenged probably needed to be in order for us to know not only what we believed, but why. (3) Never challenge Dr. Moody unless you have first researched your own question and done your homework.

This young student was obviously oblivious to all three points as I remember him quite arrogantly, almost in contempt, saying to Dr. Moody, "Can you give me any passage of scripture to substantiate your position?"

It was easy to see that Dr. Moody was a little taken back by the spirit of the question, more so than the question itself. So, some of us could not suppress our grins as Dr. Moody, shaking those bulldog jaws of his, barked in response, "name a book!"

"What?" said the student.

"Name any book and I will quote you the passage. Every book in the Bible speaks to the point that I am making. So instead of me perhaps suggesting that there is only one such text, you name the book."

I remember a book being named. Dr. Moody responded, quoting the passage verbatim that made his point. Then he said to the young man, "Name another book."

This process was repeated several more times. Then, quite humbled by both Dr. Moody and us, his classmates, who began to chuckle aloud, the young man said, "Dr. Moody, I apologize for my behavior. Your point is well taken." I do not recall the student ever challenging Dr. Moody in that manner again.

The Ultimate Step

To be asked the question, "Do the New Testament Scriptures speak of a Christian never dying alone or forsaken?" I find myself feeling and thinking, I believe, a lot like Dr. Moody. My response: "Name a book."

I am convicted there is not a book in the New Testament that does not to some degree and in some fashion affirm that Jesus Christ is the one in whom, through whom, and with whom we, as Christians, will experience eternal life beyond our physical death, in heaven.

But of all the books and all the recorded words of Christ, which passage is the most meaningful and informative to me? Which passage would best describe the experience of death, as did those individuals whose stories I have recorded? Which passage best perhaps prepares you and me for our encounter of death?

My immediate focus is known as Jesus's farewell discourse to His disciples recorded in the Gospel of John, beginning in Chapter 13:31.

The setting was the night before Jesus' crucifixion. Jesus was gathered in an upper room in a house in Jerusalem with his twelve disciples. They had worshipfully celebrated, as was their Jewish custom, the Hebrew Seder meal in observance of the Passover. The Passover, you recall, is the first of the last three great festivals in Israel's liturgical calendar--the annual feast commemorating God's deliverance of the Hebrew people from Egyptian slavery. It is celebrated, acknowledging God's subsequent giving of the Commandments through Moses at Mt. Sinai, and God's calling of the Hebrews as His chosen people, with the fulfillment of the promise of the land of Israel itself.

Upon the conclusion of the meal, Jesus told the disciples of His imminent death. Through the drinking of wine and the breaking of bread, He had symbolized His suffering and death with the promise that someday He and the disciples would be reunited around a similar table for an eternal celebration. He had commanded the disciples to likewise in the future drink the wine and eat the bread, remembering his efficacious death and the promise of their reunion. Some Christians call this practice today "The Lord's Supper." Others call the practice "Communion." Some Christians use the terms interchangeably.

Some Christians believe that this practice today is inherently efficacious, a sacrament, meaning that it is essential to salvation and has saving powers. Personally, I do not. Rather, I agree with other Christians that this observance today is an "ordinance." It is ordained by Christ as a tutor, to teach us about Him and never to allow us to forget.

But amid the institution of this act of remembrance by Jesus, something dramatic had occurred. Jesus had revealed that the final circumstances of His crucifixion and death were set in motion from that very moment in an act of betrayal by one of the twelve disciples themselves, although I am not certain, judging from my reading of the text, that the other disciples really overheard or understood all that was said and done when the betrayer was exposed. His name was Judas Iscariot. Judas fled the table to complete his overt act of betrayal that would result in Jesus's arrest at the hands of the Romans.

In time, the other disciples would betray Jesus, too. Peter, for example, would publicly deny Him and curse at the mentioning of his having any relationship with Jesus. And of all the others, not one came to his public defense. At His actual crucifixion, only John is mentioned as a disciple who was identifiably present as

Jesus entrusted His mother, Mary, and her care to him. Were the others there? We are not told.

But within this setting, following the establishment of The Lord's Supper or Communion, Jesus spoke to the disciples the words which I find most important, most significant to the question raised from the very first page of this book: "For the Christian, what is the actual death experience like? What does it entail?"

Jesus's statements, His promises, were words the disciples needed, even more than they understood at that moment. For tradition tells us that only one of them, John, called "the beloved disciple," would die as an old man at home in bed. All the others would die horrendous deaths as martyrs for Christ's sake. Indeed, they would need these words of Jesus in the future more than they could foresee.

That fact alone carries more weight for me in relationship to their value and insight than the many volumes that have been written regarding these words of Jesus as simply being given as a "see you later" expression, utilizing a traditional Hebrew formula of oral departure. I mean no criticism of those who expound these theories, I simply find no eternal or existential value in them.

Rather, my understanding is that the disciples are confused. They are pondering, "How can the promised Messiah suffer these things and leave us in this world, which in every respect seems to have changed so very little, if at all?" The disciples are also ashamed. All the issues they had fought over such as, "Who would be the greatest among them?" were surely daggers within their minds. Countless questions such as, "How could we have let this happen to Him?" surely mocked their best thoughts about themselves. The disciples were also afraid. "What is really happening?" surely covered a multitude of underlying concerns including: "What will happen to us if He is really taken from us? Will the Romans seek us out next? If everything He has done, which is all good, is culminated in only His death, what hope is there for us?"

So being confused, ashamed, and afraid, the disciples' faith is shaken, and their hopes are apparently shattered. The disciples were needing a word especially for themselves as followers of Christ.

And frankly, the preacher in me cannot help but steal a paragraph here. Who among us has not been there emotionally, spiritually, if not physically? I surely have been and am convinced that every human being on this earth, if they are honest, would have to admit the same. Confusion, shame, and fear--they are formidable enemies and universally experienced. In the face of death, this fact is never more evident. No wonder so many people opt for death rather than to confront these realities and, through Christ, opt for life.

Well, excuse the preaching, but if you can identify with these thoughts and feelings of confusion, shame and fear, then you can put yourself in the room with the disciples to whom Jesus spoke that night before His crucifixion.

But how do we know that the disciples thought and felt these things? The golden text for me begins in John 14:1. Jesus puts all the disciples' thoughts and feelings out on the table in his very first statement (verse 1a RSV), "Let not your hearts be troubled."

Understanding the challenges of translating this verse, I prefer reading it this way, "No longer let your hearts be troubled." I do not believe that Jesus was telling them not to become troubled, they already were. He was giving them reaffirmation and renewed hope amid their trouble. The depth of their confusion, shame and fear was almost unfathomable as noted in the term translated "heart," a word here meaning the very core of one's faith, emotion, and thought.

One would think that by now the disciples would have learned that nothing in their souls could be hidden from Jesus, and that there was no dimension within their souls about which Jesus was not lovingly concerned. Maybe they did. But regardless, the playing field was now level with everything exposed. All this became undeniable when Jesus said, "No longer, not even in the face of death, let your heart be troubled." (John 14:1a personal translation).

Then He stated why they, the disciples, no longer needed to be so troubled. His answer? "Me!" said He, "You believe in God, believe also in Me!" (14:1b, RSV). The imperative here is also the progressive meaning: "You have trusted and have believed in God; you have trusted and believed in Me; keep on trusting and keep on believing!"

Jesus would explain this in even fuller detail using specific analogies such as the vine and its branches. But here, still at the table, He would be quick to explain why the disciples should keep on trusting and believing especially in the face of the imminent reality of death.

Here is where the words of Jesus in the text align perfectly with the lives, the words, the visions, and the legacies of Uncle Bud, Mr. Charles, Nana, Sis, Old Joe, Kay, Mr. George, John and a host of others whose stories I have not written in this book.

Citing perhaps the most familiar translation of this text in The King James Version, Jesus said, "In my Father's house are many mansions; if it were not so, I would have told you. I go to prepare a place for you…" (John 14:2 KJV).

There was no mistaking what Jesus was saying in the minds of the disciples, "Beyond death, there is an existence. There is a specific place. There is a heavenly realm in which God abides and where those people who follow Christ will abide. It is a special place because God and Jesus are there. But it has even within it a special unique place for you." Said Jesus, "Prepared by Me, for you!"

Now I must admit that, as a boy, growing up in a very rural area within a family of limited means and formal education, and in a little white-boarded church where the pastors'--as marvelous as they were, and they were—had little formal theological education, I thought that Jesus was promising me a palatial estate that would make Buckingham Palace look like a back yard tool shed. I cannot help but grin even as I write these words to think that I held such an image for so long.

But now, I believe that I understand more rightly, although the mystery this side of heaven will surely remain unfathomable. I believe that when Jesus spoke of "mansions" within my Father's house, He was not alluding so much to social distancing as He was to intimacy.

Little debate surrounds the interpretation of the word "mansions" within our culture. The word translated in 1611 A.D. as "mansions" is perhaps better understood as "rooms." After all, the statement begins with, "*Within* my Father's house," not outside, around, amid, but *within*.

However, this is not to suggest the space or limited accommodation of some cosmic Motel 6 or Econo Inn. The idea seems more to be what we would imagine as a plush, roomy, comfortable apartment complex with more than ample space to fulfill our Lord's creative intent for us while affording that intimacy with Him-- which is at the heart of our deepest wants and needs.

If I might use my imagination, I would perceive that space to be my own plot within God's expansive Garden of Eden. Not too large, not too small, but just right, especially for those intimate walks in the cool of the day.

I am deeply indebted again to Rabbi Peli of Jerusalem in part for this image. He was lecturing one evening on the Jewish view of the creation narratives. He stated his belief that the controversy or debate between the world of science that holds to Darwin's theories regarding evolution and "the big bang," and the Biblical view of creation based solely on the creation stories of Genesis chapter 1:1-2:4a and chapter 2:4b-25, is in one sense, "absurd."

For the Biblical accounts of creation, he said, were not and are not scientific documents that can be validated or invalidated. The biblical accounts of creation for the Jews were and are "faith" documents.

Regardless of how one might interpret any one term, or collection of terms, within the creation stories such as the often hotly debated Hebrew "Yam," translated "day," or the Hebrew term "Adam" translated "mankind" or transliterated as "Adam," the ultimate meaning of the creation stories remains the same.

He illustrated his point citing an intersection of five streets merging in the city of Jerusalem. "As a tourist who does not speak the language," he said, "you have written instructions of each street you are to follow to get to your desired destination.

"And according to those instructions," he further explained, "at this intersection of merging streets, you must alter your route and take a different street. But here is where you encounter a grand problem. You look for the street signpost which would normally advise you of the right direction.

"However, the street signpost is not in its place. A city bus has ripped it from its base. It is lying up against one of the store front businesses just off the walk-way curb."

Then the Rabbi asked, "Not being able to ask anyone for help because you do not speak the language, with no availability of communication with anyone but yourself, what do you do? How do you know which way is the correct route for you to proceed?"

I still recall that not one of us listening to his lecture responded to his question, although he paused for a response. He finally challenged our silence with this comment: "Surely you know, any boy scout can answer the question." By the way, I am an Eagle Scout, but I was not about to try to speak for the rabbi.

Then most seriously, he gave us the answer. He said, "You have your written instructions that include one most vital bit of information. You can read it and know it to be true. You know upon arriving at this intersection where you came from.

"Knowing this, you walk over and pick up the street signpost. You stand it again where it once stood. You rightly align the street signpost by having it rightly reflect the one thing you do know: where you came from. Then you can look to the street signpost and know the right way to go. It is always important to know and remember from where you have come as you are seeking your way forward.

"The creation stories," the rabbi continued with great emotion, "tell us where we came from. They tell us foremost that in the beginning we came out of the mind, heart, and will of God created to live in communion with Him as a creature who loves his Creator and is beloved by his Creator.

"But something dreadful happened." The creature and the creator, man and God, became separated as reflected in God's question, 'Adam, where are you?'

"It is of infinite importance to understand this about the creation narratives: They are telling us where we came from, where our home originally once was, so that we might rightly interpret the remainder of Holy Scripture that is trying to tell us how to get back there!"

I was awed when the rabbi explained the creation narratives in this way forty years ago. I am even more awed today. I am still awed when I hear through the writer John, Jesus saying almost in response to the analogy of Rabbi Peli, "That place for which you have been searching, that Edenic home, is real. And you, through Me, have a place in it!"

So, call it a mansion, or room, or a garden plot, or whatever you will. But perhaps the greatest word is "home." Jesus said, "No longer let your heart be troubled, through all of this you are still headed home" (John 14:1ff paraphrase).

No wonder Mr. Charles, though overjoyed, seemed a bit perplexed when he asked, "Don't you hear the music?" No wonder Nana wept when she said, "He says that I have to wait three days. But the flowers are so beautiful. I don't want to wait. I want to go now!" No wonder all the others whose stories I've recorded said, "It's okay! It is really, really, okay!" They were hearing and seeing what none of us yet have seen, but as Christians will see; the sights and sounds of home.

But back to the scriptures. According to John, after calming and reassuring the disciples, after reaffirming the reality of heaven and their special place within it, which He, Jesus Himself, will prepare for them, He added what to me is the preeminent promise: "And when I go and prepare (that) place for you, I will come again and will take you to Myself, that where I am you may be also." (John 14:3 RSV).

Could this really have meant that Jesus Himself would come back to personally reunite with His disciples at their moment of death to personally escort them to their heavenly home? That is what He says! Will He do the same for all His disciples including you and me? Indeed, I am convinced that is the meaning of the text.

Disciples of Jesus need not fear, or be "soul" troubled, because even in the face of death Jesus says, "I will take you to myself." Or in other words, "I will be with you." It sounds a lot like what David, the Psalmist, said concerning the "valley of the shadow of death," does it not?"

But is not Jesus talking about His second coming here? One might quickly ask several questions: "Is He not talking about what Christians call the 'parousia'? Is He not talking about that occasion when He will return to the earth and time itself will be no more as the great eschaton will have arrived? Is He not talking about that day the Apostle Paul described to the Christians at Corinth when He said, 'Lo, I tell you a mystery: We shall not sleep but we shall all be changed…in a moment, in the twinkling of an eye, at the last trumpet. For the trumpet will sound and the dead will be raised imperishable, and we shall be changed. For this perishable nature must put on the imperishable, and the mortal put on immorality, then shall come to pass the saying that is written,

'Death is swallowed up in victory. O death where is thy victory? O death, where is thy sting? The sting of death is sin, and the power of sin is the law. But thanks be to God who gives us the victory through our Lord Jesus Christ'" (1 Corinthians 15:51-57 RSV).

My answer is, "Yes." Jesus is making this promise to His disciples, to all of us who believe in Him, with that day in mind. I do not doubt that fact. I believe in the bodily second coming of Jesus Christ whereupon, as Paul said to the Christians in Rome, "Every knee shall bow and every tongue confess that Jesus Christ is Lord" (Romans 14:11 paraphrase).

But while casting no shadow of doubt upon that day, against the backdrop of the old question, "By where do the dead abide until that great reunion day of all Christians;" in light of the Apostle Paul's statement to the Christians at Corinth that to be "away from the body" is to be "at home with the Lord." (II Corinthians 5:6 RSV); and given the witness of so many Christians over the years, including the few recorded in this book; I must ask, "Is there not more here than simply a foretelling of a cosmic day yet to come of which only God, Himself knows the time?" (see I Thessalonians 5:1ff).

I have come to believe there is. When Jesus said, "And when I go and prepare (that) place for you, I will come again and take you to Myself, that where I am you may be also"(John14:3 RSV), I do not believe as once I did that He was speaking merely in analogy, simile or metaphor. Rather, I believe He was speaking literally. I believe He was speaking personally. I believe He meant every word exactly as He said it.

Although my mind cannot fully comprehend it, I am

convinced this much is true. At the moment of our death, we will immediately share with Christ one among many commonalities. With Him, there will be no more boundaries of time and space. There will be no more minutes, hours, days, months, or years. Only eternity.

And since time is no longer a qualifier, could even our death, given what Jesus said, be but the beginning of our great personal parousia experience? I believe so.

Or to put it most simply, based on the many witnesses during my life; based upon the Holy Scriptures, both the Old and the New Testaments; based specifically on what Jesus said to the disciples the night before His own crucifixion and death; What happens at the moment of a Christian's death?

Jesus Himself comes! As a friend, a brother, the Lord, the Savior, God… Jesus Himself comes! He does not send ahead for His disciples or for you and me as His disciples. He does not send an angel to fetch us. He does not just meet us along the way.

Jesus Himself comes! Said He, "I will come…and receive (or get) you." (John 14:3 RSV). Jesus comes whereby, not one of His disciples dies, not you or I, alone or forsaken. Therefore, death becomes with Jesus, but a relocating, a movement, from this world as we know it to that heavenly place He has designed and prepared specifically for us, with Him.

The words of my friends echo in my mind still again: "He says it is time for me to go with Him…He says that He will be back for me in three days…He says that I will be going home with Him before morning…He says that He will return soon for me and that everything is okay."

I find no New Testament scriptures that would refute such

dying declarations of faith, love, and hope. I do find a multitude of texts trying to direct me, you and a lost world through, and in the person of Jesus Christ, back into a perfect communion with God--as even the rabbi said, "Back home."

Death is a journey with Jesus back home.

CHAPTER 12

THE ULTIMATE STEP

In the preceding chapters I have shared from my years of vocational ministry a few of my intimate moments with others as they experienced both the anticipation and the reality of their personal death. I have looked to the Holy Scriptures for validation of and insight into their testimonies of visions and sounds. While doing so, I have reflected upon my own mortality and how I might yet minister more effectively to the grieving and dying I am encountering and will yet encounter. And I find myself asking, "Now how do I bring all of this information, insight, and reflection together to fulfill my originally stated purpose?"

As originally explained, my purpose has been not to write a theological tome, which this brief collection of thoughts certainly is not. My purpose has not been to produce a scholarly essay for which I avow no such authority or wisdom. My purpose has not been to stake any claim to a "new" epiphany or original insight, having read and heard similar testimonies of many others on the reality of death over my almost seven decades. My stated purpose has been simply to address from a personal, pastoral point of view the question, "What does the death of a Christian entail? What does the Christian experience at the moment of death?"

I must give credit to a dear friend, Steven Ayers, from Hartwell, Georgia, for just last evening giving me the direction I needed when discussing this very subject with him on the telephone. He suggested, "Why don't you just give a simple, concluding definition of death and put it in a story the way Jesus did? After all, that is how you have effectively concluded every sermon I have ever heard you preach."

The wisdom of his statement was apparent from the moment he said it. That is exactly what Jesus, the Master Teacher, did. When Jesus sought to emphasize a great truth, He told a story. Sometimes Jesus used a narrative such as that of the "Good Samaritan" (Luke 10:30 ff). Still, at other times, he used a parable such as that of the "prodigal sons" (Luke 15:11 ff). But either way, Jesus most often told a story. He kept it simple.

What is my simple definition of the death experience of a Christian? My definition is, and I state it most reverently: Death is the "one ultimate step." It is the one ultimate step of faith in obedience to Jesus Christ. Death is the experience of Jesus coming to the Christian, to you and me as Christians, saying to us what He said long ago to His originally chosen twelve disciples, "Follow Me. Come with Me."

At our death as Christians, we take that one ultimate step by saying, "Yes, Lord. I will come with You." In that one ultimate step we step out of this physical world of time and space into the divine world of eternity where Jesus prepared a special place especially for us—a place inclusive of Him, the Father, our loved

The Ultimate Step

ones and a host of others we will have an eternity to get to know and love. Death is that one ultimate step.

What will death for a Christian be like? Ah…the story. I have personally visited the site in the city of Jerusalem on several occasions. On two of those occasions I not only viewed the site from the outside of its locked iron gated entrance, but gaining access to the keys that allowed me and the others with me to pass through by "sharing a few shekels" with the Arab gatekeeper who lived just up the hill, I was able to enter the site and experience its history as only a small percentage of the visitors to Jerusalem I understand still do.

I refer to Hezekiah's tunnel. I cannot speak to any changes that might have occurred at the site since my last visit many years ago, although I have had others tell me since that little has changed. At the time of my last visit to the site, some years later than my original visit, the iron gate did restrict most visitors from entering for a very good reason: the tunnel had hardly been altered except for a few occasions of being dredged since the day it was dug. Because of its risks, some people died in their efforts to walk the length of it.

Where and what is Hezekiah's tunnel? It is in Jerusalem, Israel. It is in the southeastern area of the Kidron Valley. In the side of the valley is a small cavern within which is Gihon Spring, the ancient primary water source for the people of Jerusalem. During the reign of King Hezekiah of Jerusalem, it became necessary by the order of the King to reroute the flow of water from the spring by the digging of an aqueduct, specifically a tunnel, hence the name: Hezekiah's Tunnel. So, by hand, the tunnel was dug. (see II Kings 20:20)

It was dug in a hurry. King Hezekiah, and Israel apparently as a whole, knew of the threat of the Assyrian invaders. Hezekiah was evidently urged to reinforce his fortifications and prepare for just such a siege.

One of Hezekiah's major concerns was, should a siege occur, an adequate water supply for the city. But the problem was this: the primary water source, Gihon Spring, was actually "outside" the old city wall. Should the Assyrians locate and overtake Gihon Spring, they could literally thirst Jerusalem into defeat, and worse still, into annihilation. The Assyrians were known not only for defeating an enemy, but also annihilating it. Often, after defeating a foe, the Assyrians would separate families, clans and tribes, only then to deport their defeated enemies to other locations, forcing them to interbreed, thereby eliminating a race of people by creating another in its place.

Hezekiah knew that Gihon Spring had led to Jerusalem's defeat previously (See II Samuel 5:6ff). It was precisely at Gihon Spring that David had sent his guerilla fighters by night up the old water shaft into the city from which they captured the infiltrated city the next day. They defied the idea that the old city was unconquerable, that even a "blind man" could defend it.

So, Hezekiah knew that the primary water source had to be protected. His plan was both simple and complex at the same time. The plan was simple in that its goal was to bring the water source under protective custody. Keep it available to the people within the city while concealing it from the enemy and eliminating the vulnerability of the old water shaft.

But the implementation was complex. It has been described to me by some of the giants in engineering as an engineering marvel, even a miracle of the ancient world. The implementation involved the digging of a tunnel, a literal aqueduct, from Gihon Spring outside the eastern city wall, underneath the city wall through solid rock to a pool or reservoir located toward the western side of the city. The completed aqueduct, or tunnel, would be 1749 feet long or approximately one-third of a mile, although the completed distance was not dictated by the location of the reservoir as much as it was dictated by the expedience with which the tunnel had to be dug.

You see, compounding the need for expediency were two underlying challenges which were critical. The first challenge was the necessity of the gravity flow of the water from the spring to the pool or reservoir. The second challenge was the need to dig through the softer limestone rather than harder rock. Meeting these challenges without the need for expediency were feats in themselves. But the zigzagging, or "S" shape of the tunnel, is even more exaggerated because, in the effort to rush the tunnel's completion, the tunnel was not simply dug in one direction, from the spring to the reservoir or vise-versa. Rather, men with picks began digging from both directions, from the spring and the pool, hoping to intersect with each other somewhere in the process.

Miraculously, they did. As a result, the zigs and zags resulted in the longer tunnel. But the erratic nature of the stone through which they were digging, along with the need for gravity flow, resulted in further distinctive traits of the tunnel.

The tunnel itself is not consistent in height or width. Neither is the water flowing through it consistent in depth due to both the tunnel construction and the gushing of the water from the spring.

I stand six feet, four inches tall. I was thin then, as I have become now in my older age. I found the tunnel at times to be comfortably wide. At other times, I found myself turning sideways to sidestep my way through.

At some places I could not begin to guess the height of the high ceiling above me. At other places I was forced to bend and kneel low to pass through. At some points, the water level was shin high, while at other times, especially when bent over, I felt fortunate to keep my head above water. It is no wonder that people have drowned in this tunnel.

Of course, no lighting within the tunnel existed. And walking was not easy on the feet. No massive removal of the stones over which the water has flowed for centuries had occurred, in my opinion, since the day the tunnel was dug. No convenient walkway over the water had been constructed as had been done in a similar tunnel in the ruins of the old northern city of Megiddo. The footing was-- and I am told still is--treacherous.

Hezekiah is remembered for numerous reasons among the Kings of Israel. One of his greatest building achievements was the digging of this tunnel so that the people of Jerusalem could withstand any assault by an enemy with an ample supply of spring water.

The tunnel would also provide other advantages as products of wartime often do. For example, it would provide water for an irrigation system that would aid in the economy. But it served its primary purpose well. Jerusalem never fell to Assyria or any other invader due to the lack of drinking water. But given my purpose here, I have gone in some detail in my attempt to describe both the history and the atmosphere of Hezekiah's tunnel for still another reason.

If it is possible for you as the reader to do so, I would like for you to envision this tunnel with me. I would also like for you to go there in your mind. Step down at the entrance of the tunnel into the cold water, feeling its chill as well as the infirm footing of the varied stones beneath the surface. Peek into the pitch-black dark, damp, winding tunnel ahead of you with only a faint, lit candle in your hand. That is how both my visits through the tunnel began.

It is precisely that setting that can aid us all in understanding what death for every Christian is like.

You see, for some Christians, the experience of death is like Tom's experience, and more like my first visit, to Hezekiah's tunnel. I am indebted to Dr. Bruce Morgan, my mentor, whom I hold in the highest esteem to this day, for Tom's story. Tom would visit Hezekiah's tunnel not long after my first visit to the site.

Tom was the pastor of a growing suburban church. The church was growing under his leadership, but at the time of Tom's "tunnel experience" the church had also become bogged down in a building program which was causing stress within the congregation. But the stress within the membership of the church, as significant as it was, did not begin to reflect the level of stress that the entire dilemma was creating within Tom.

Tom had all the classic symptoms of uncontrolled stress; the inability to sleep, change of appetite, difficulty performing routine tasks, anxiety attacks, shortness of breath, and chest pains.

Tom's physician recommended that he take some time away from work to afford his body and spirit the distance from the source of his stress and the time required for healing and renewal. But Tom, like most dedicated pastors I know, kept putting the needs of others ahead of his own, as unwise as such an action is.

Even a well of water cannot slake the thirst of people if it does find the time and opportunity to replenish its own resources.

So, it was Tom's wife who, knowing his family's history of angina and his boundless workaholism, surprised him with a prearranged trip to visit Israel with a group of other ministers in hopes that he would regain both his health and energy. I might add with my tongue (or pen) in my cheek, as my mentor said it: "Her intentions were good, although her strategy was questionable."

Initially, the first several days, Tom relaxed. But then it happened. As Tom and the group of clergy, with whom he traveled along with their tour guide, was standing on the pinnacle of the Mount of Olives overlooking the Kidron Valley and the city of Jerusalem, the tour guide said, "If you look toward the southern end of the valley near the old Eastern wall, you will see the area in which there is hidden in the soil, a cave which leads into Gihon Spring and from the Spring into a place known as Hezekiah's tunnel!"

The guide related the history of the spring and the purpose of Hezekiah's tunnel, including one facet of its history that I have yet to mention. He told how the reservoir at the end of Hezekiah's tunnel inside the Old City was named "the pool of Siloam," as it is known in the New Testament (see John 9:1FF) where it is recorded that Jesus met a man who had been blind from birth. The disciples had inquired, "Master, who sinned, this man or his parents that he was born blind?"

Jesus had explained, "Neither, but that God's works might be revealed." Then in fulfillment of His own words, Jesus had taken clay from the ground, spat upon it, and placed the moistened mixture over the blind man's eyes. Then Jesus told the man, "Go,

The Ultimate Step

wash in the pool of Siloam." And the man did so. And immediately he could see with his physical eyes.

But the man found something else that day greater than mere eyesight. He gained spiritual insight. In Christ he found his salvation. "That happened," said the tour guide, "at the end of Hezekiah's tunnel at the reservoir known as the Pool of Siloam."

Well, that did it. Suddenly all the ministers in the group began to question the guide. "We know it is late in the afternoon. Is it possible for us to visit this place, perhaps even, although it is not part of our itinerary, to walk inside the tunnel?" Obviously, this tour guide, knowing the same little Arab with the keys and perhaps wanting a generous tip, said, "I will see if I can arrange it. I cannot promise, but I will try."

The tour guide succeeded. So shortly thereafter, there was Tom…standing in the gushing, cold water up to his knees, staring into the pitch black darkness of the entrance into an erratic winding tunnel, trying to keep his balance while standing on the slippery, jagged rocks beneath the surface of the water. And his stress level had never been higher.

It was for Tom, by his own confession, the darkness that triggered the renewal of his stress, or should I write, dis-stress. But among the group of ministers and the tour guide, there were two flashlights that afforded Tom some reassurance.

The group simply decided to walk through the tunnel in single file with one man with a flashlight leading the way and another man with a flashlight bringing up the rear. It was a good plan, at least in the beginning.

But Tom, deep into the tunnel where the walls get close and the water gets high, stumbled, and lost his shoe. For reasons never explained, he was passed by the last man with a flashlight. Tom became even more anxious and afraid as, trying to get himself together, he fell farther and farther behind.

Then it happened. The tunnel twisted and suddenly Tom found himself in total darkness and in total silence as he could no longer hear the voices of the others who had walked ahead of him. To say that Tom felt horribly and dreadfully alone, forsaken in the dark, was an understatement.

But feeling his way through the tunnel, Tom attempted to proceed, fighting absolute panic with every breath, thinking, as he described it, "I must not faint, lest I drown here never to be found." The only voice that kept speaking to him was that of his own pounding heartbeat and elevated pulse rate repeating, "Tom's Tomb…Tom's Tomb…Tom's Tomb."

At the precise moment when Tom thought his one breath was his last, there appeared a little Palestinian child about nine or ten years old with a lighted candle. For reasons Tom never explained, perhaps never knew, on the western side of the tunnel the boy climbed over the barrier that forbids people from entering the tunnel at the pool, as does the iron gate at Gihon Spring to the east.

The boy, who spoke no English, reached out to Tom, took his hand, and literally tugged him to the light, freedom, and life of Siloam's pool. "I laid there for a while," Tom said, "contemplating the entire event and my response to it, until, like the blind man Jesus healed and saved, I could go on my way rejoicing."

Dr. Morgan, in telling Tom's story, made this astute observation: "Isn't it interesting that the Hebrew word for salvation is 'Yah Sha,' meaning that God will lead us to a wide-open space with room to breathe."

For some Christians, the death experience is like Tom's experience in Hezekiah's Tunnel and, admittedly, my first visit to the site. To varying degrees, the fear is real. The anxiety is undeniable. To varying degrees, the idea of closing one's eyes to an unknown darkness is foreboding.

But still again, the testimony of those whose stories I have told confirm the witness of the Holy Spirit and the promise of Jesus Himself within the heart of the Christian: "When you breathe your last physical breath, when you close your eyes toward the darkness of this earth and life you leave behind, like the little Palestinian boy I will come to you. I will not be carrying a light because I am the light. I will take that one ultimate step of death with you. I will lead you to the light, freedom, and eternal life of heaven itself within which is your special prepared place waiting just for you!"

So, to Christians like Tom, the one word that comes to mind is, "Do not let your heart any longer be troubled!"

But for other Christians, death will be more like my second visit to Hezekiah's Tunnel. I believe I speak for most Christians in describing the experience this way: The moment will be more akin to those individuals' whose experiences I have recounted in this book.

You see, the second time I visited Hezekiah's Tunnel, although the tunnel's geological construction with its challenges and risks had not changed, the tunnel experience was drastically and wonderfully different. Yes, the water was still very cold as it flowed and gushed from the Spring of Gihon to Siloam's pool. The rocky base upon which I had to walk was still slippery and inconsistent beneath the surface of the water. The pitch-black darkness of the winding tunnel ahead still confronted me with its most formidable, foreboding, and threatening pose. The small lighted candle in my hand still offered only limited vision and cast the most intimidating of shadows. But on this occasion, this second visit to Hezekiah's Tunnel, one marvelous difference existed that enabled me, with confidence, to learn, grow, and more fully celebrate the experience from its very first step.

The difference was simply this: This second experience of Hezekiah's tunnel had within it not even the slightest modicum of fear. Absolutely no fear! I had been this way before. I knew exactly what to expect. I knew that varying my posture and lengthening my strides were necessary to traverse the tunnel.

But what perhaps most eliminated my fear was this: I knew on this occasion what was awaiting me, and the others whom I was leading through the tunnel, at the other end.

I could envision Siloam's pool. I could anticipate the joy one feels as the light of the sun literally welcomes you to this ancient oasis within the city. The anticipation of what I knew and the confidence of knowing the way from where I was to there, assuaged the fear, transplanting it with peace, joy and even a degree of eagerness. In so doing, it enabled me to more experience the walk through the tunnel itself as a source of further educational insight and spiritual growth. So, when I took my second step into the darkness and challenges of Hezekiah's tunnel, it was still a big step, but not an ominous one. Should someone had asked me then, "Are you sure, understanding the risks that you want to do this?" I would have responded, "It's okay. I am at peace. You tell anybody and everybody that might be concerned that it is all okay!"

The Ultimate Step

I am convinced that for most Christians that is how one might understand and describe the death experience. It still entails unknowns. But what Christians do know alleviates all fear. They know what awaits them on the other side of the death experience. Through the prism of the Holy Spirit of Jesus Christ within them, they have already had glimpses of it.

These Christians have prayed as Jesus taught them in the model prayer, "Our Father who art in Heaven, hallowed be thy name, thy kingdom come, thy will be done, on earth as it is in heaven" (Matthew 6:9ff KJV). And as a result, they have witnessed occasions when they knew it to be true, that Heaven had transcended, if only for a brief encounter.

That is why when given visions, certain individuals could confidently say, "I have seen heaven!" They recognized it. Before they took that one ultimate step with Christ into heaven, a little bit of heaven had already gotten into them.

The Apostle Paul said, "For me to live is Christ, and to die is gain (Philippians 1:21 RSV). How could he say such a thing? Because he knew what awaited him. He knew that his one ultimate step with Christ at the moment of his death would be but an exit from here to there, into heaven itself. Many Christians, like Paul, do not fear death because they foresee and desire the experience of heaven.

But there was another reason I did not fear my second experience of walking through Hezekiah's tunnel. I knew the way. I understood already the challenges of not letting my candle be extinguished along the route. I knew already that the markings of the old water shaft, the hollow of the cave wall from which ancient inscriptions were taken, the narrowing and low areas were all landmarks of the progress of one's passage. I understood the twists and turns and had no need to be confused or threatened by them. Again…I knew the way. Therefore, I had no need to fear.

I am convinced that most Christians face that one ultimate step or actual moment of their death when Jesus comes without fear for the same reason.

Simply, they know "the way!" In fact, Jesus described Himself using these very words. On the same night Jesus promised the disciples that He would prepare that very special place in heaven for all his disciples and He would personally come again to receive them and take them there, it was Thomas who asked him, "But Lord…we do not know where you are going (e.g., where heaven is); how can we know the way?" to which Jesus responded, "I am the way…" (John 14:5ff RSV).

At the moment of death when Jesus comes to the Christian, the Christian can confidently, without fear, go with Jesus. And this is true not only because Jesus is the one, ultimate means of access to God the Father and heaven (John 14:6), but because Jesus has been this way before. That being true, Jesus not only understands what, out of love, He is doing for us, but further He understands all that is happening within us. Frankly, I think that is why He personally comes for us.

Jesus is the way. Jesus knows the way. And the Christian who has spent time in prayer and fellowship with Jesus in his devotional life and lifestyle has no fear of Jesus's coming, whenever that might be. For when Jesus comes, recognition is not, nor will it be a problem, because the Christian and Christ will have spent time together already. Only the venue and the depth of intimacy with insight is altered…and gloriously so.

The Ultimate Step

All the stories of my friends and family members leaving for heaven had that one experience in common. Again, surely you heard it. Upon seeing Jesus, the way, they had no fear and wanted to go with Him.

I have said on some occasions that given a person's faith and circumstances of poor health and constant suffering, that death sometimes comes as a friend. I do not think that reflecting upon all the experiences I have encountered with death, including those described in these pages, that I shall ever say that again.

Why? Because my statement is in error. The statement is too limited. Death for a Christian does not "sometimes" come as a friend. Death *always* comes as a friend, in a friend, and through a friend. His name is Jesus. Maybe that is at least in part what Jesus was saying to his disciples when He said on that same night before his crucifixion and death, "No longer do I call you servants…(rather) I call you my friends" (see John 15:15ff).

That is why when speaking to most Christians about the possibility of their death, one will hear a similar response to the question "But what if all does not go well?" to that which I was given by a dear friend, Henry Brown, who facing a difficult surgery to remove his cancerous tumor, said, "Live or die, because of Jesus, either way, I win!"

I did not fear my second walk through Hezekiah's Tunnel, because I knew what was awaiting me at the end, and I knew the way. Most Christians do not fear the moment of their death for the same reasons.

Of course, all this being true, on both visits to Hezekiah's Tunnel, there was one constant. Given my anxiety, or given my lack of it, it was still required of me to take that initial step. I still had to step down into the gushing water. I still had to step into the dark, foreboding tunnel. I still had to step forward in the faith that I would not be disappointed.

Likewise, when at the moment of death Jesus comes, and He stretches out His hand to the Christian saying, "It is time. Come with me," how does the experience, the journey, actually begin?

The experience begins with that one ultimate step of unreserved faith and obedience summed up in this, "Yes, Lord let's go!"...the very same act of trust and obedience with which the Christian journey begins upon the occasion of one's initial conversion or, as some people rightly describe it, "the salvation experience."

To press the point, I am writing of that spiritual rebirth that has occurred, or yet will occur, when in response to Jesus' call to us to repent of our sin, to embrace and trust His saving grace, to invite Him in His Spirit to reign in our hearts as Savior and Lord, taking up permanent residence there, and to follow Him in obedience wherever He might lead, we say, "Yes, Lord, let's go!"

Perhaps no one could say it better that did John H. Sammis in 1887 when he penned the words to the old Christian hymn that as a boy I sang so often during worship at the "Rehobeth Baptist" country church:

> *"When we walk with the Lord*
> *In the light of His word,*
> *What a glory He sheds on our way!*
> *While we do His good will,*
> *He abides with us still,*
> *And with all who will trust and obey."*

Trust and obey for there's no other way,
To be happy in Jesus, than to trust and obey.
Not a burden we bear,
Not a sorrow we share,
But our toil He doth richly repay;
Not a grief or a loss,
Not a frown or a cross,
But is blest if we trust and obey."
Trust and obey for there's no other way,
To be happy in Jesus, than to trust and obey.
"But we never can prove
The delights of His love
Until all on the altar we lay;
For the favor He shows,
For the joy He bestows,
Are for them who will trust and obey."
Trust and obey for there's no other way,
To be happy in Jesus, than to trust and obey.
"Then in fellowship sweet
We will sit at His feet,
Or we'll walk by His side in the way;
What He says we will do;
Where he sends we will go;
Never fear, only trust and obey."
Trust and obey for there's no other way,
To be happy in Jesus, than to trust and obey.

'Death is that one ultimate step of trust and obedience that confirms and completes a Christian's salvation experience. Thanks be to God that we do not as Christians take that ultimate step alone or forsaken.

How fitting it is that I lay down my pen having completed the rough draft of this book on April 12, 2020…Easter Sunday…The day when Christians around the world celebrate resurrection. But this Easter is also a day when the world is facing a pandemic and the nation of the United States of America is under the quarantine of the COVID19 virus, a day during which my wife and I await the news of the imminent death of her mother due to the virus.

But Easter is not diminished, rather for my wife and me it is accentuated as the joke is on the virus and even death. We can hear her mother saying even as she labors for breath as I have heard others declare who have preceded us, "As a Christian I am not, nor shall I be alone. I am not, nor shall I be forsaken. It's okay. Tell everybody that it's okay."

"It's really okay."

Epilogue:
Unfinished Business
Follow-up Questions from the Critics

Critics are never in short supply, even loving ones. Thanks be to God for them. They serve an invaluable purpose. I write this sincerely with absolutely no sarcasm. For my use of the term "critic" is not intended to cast even the faintest shadow of negativity upon any one of them. Rather, the critic I have in mind is the person who honestly and forthrightly raises valuable questions about significant issues that otherwise might never have been asked, but needed to be considered.

For instance, given my stated conviction that death for a Christian is an experience of Jesus himself coming personally to take him or her to their specially prepared heavenly place with Him and God, the Father, one critic might ask: "But what about 'sudden' death experiences? It is one thing to die in bed anticipating that moment, but another thing to be killed instantly in an automobile accident. It is another thing to be fatally injured while performing some arduous task. It is still another thing to be randomly killed by the carelessness or intentional action of another human being. It is still another thing simply to succumb to a physical trauma such as a stroke or heart attack.

How does the idea of any circumstance of sudden, unanticipated death affect your interpretation?"

My response is, "The reality of sudden, unanticipated death

does not alter my view at all." I repeat my conviction that of the realities the moment of death facilitates, death releases us from the qualifiers of time and space. I think we perhaps are given indicators of this by people who amid trauma have said, "Time seemed to stop. It was as if all of my life flashed in slow motion before my very eyes." It does not stretch my mind to believe that Jesus still comes, whatever the circumstances this side of heaven, however we might experience them. To think of a sudden death only brings to my mind how the Apostle Paul used the word "sudden" as he described Jesus's climatic second coming as a "sudden... surprise" ...even "as a thief" (see I Thessalonians 5). Even amid the circumstance of sudden unanticipated death, no Christian dies alone, forgotten, or forsaken.

I am also thankful for the critic who would also ask this: "But what about the legions of people, Christian and non-Christian individuals, who claim to have experienced 'near death' experiences and in their visions saw nothing of Jesus Christ or heaven? What about those people who had a vision of heaven and loved ones, but did not see Jesus?"

I am very aware of what is commonly called a "near death" experience. I do not claim to have had such an extraordinary experience myself, although I have been told I was near death on several occasions. But I have known numerous individuals, including my mother, who have had such experiences, shared them openly, and who, to this day, still seek to understand their meaning.

I do not doubt the reality of such experiences. It is not my purpose here to argue their authenticity or to attempt to interpret them. I will note that the images described to me by individuals who have had these experiences have for the vast majority been wonderfully informative, inspiring, and affirming. Only for a few of these individuals has the experience had its horrors.

The vast majority for whom the experience has been affirming have described common images of bright light, tunnels, other people including loved ones who have previously died, and heavenly beings. A number have described "out of body experiences" during which they watched and overheard activities and discussions that occurred amid their lifeless bodies. Their versions and accounting of these events, including their accounting of specific conversations, were later validated to be true. If one common denominator exists among these experiences, it would be the description of an infinite love and indescribable peace.

No two of these experiences, although similarities exist, have been identical.

Some people found their near-death experience horrendous, but only as a prelude to what they described interestingly as a "wakeup call." They described the experience as a prelude to faith, to a greater appreciation of life, to a new dimension of relationships. Some believed they had seen hell as a warning from God not to take up residence there. Their common images have included ethereal escorts, dark shadows, intense suffering, and a great gift of another opportunity for a heavenly existence.

Again, it is not my purpose here to dissect, debate or interpret these experiences. But how do these experiences reflect on my belief that death is an experience of Jesus, Himself, coming to us, to escort us to that special place He has prepared for us in heaven?

My response is that these near-death experiences do not alter my belief at all. For as valuable to an individual as these near-death experiences may be, that is exactly what they are. They are near-death experiences. They are not death-experiences. The people I have known and who have shared with me of their "visitation," of Jesus coming and saying to them that it was now time to come to Him, did die. The great common experience of these people who have had near-death experiences has been their awareness and experience of infinite love and indescribable peace, but the grand difference compared to those individuals who died remains the presence of Jesus Himself.

I have read no convincing study, scientific or otherwise, that would lead me to discount or devalue a near-death experience. I have concluded that by and large such experiences are an epiphany: a message from God revealing to an individual that which he or she needs to see and understand for a more effective lifestyle. They challenge the person to live the remainder of his or her life on this earth congruent with God's creative intent invested in them.

But actual death? Again…for a Christian it is the "fulfillment" of a life lived congruent with God's creative intent invested in him or her. Time on earth is over. Death is the "fulfillment" of a life celebrated and rewarded in Christ who comes personally to take him or her home.

I am further grateful to the critic who asks, "But are you not suggesting that Christians do not really die?" My answer is, "No!" Christians do die. Their bodies die and decay. Only a blind fool would deny that fact. But the critic might say, "But what about the spirit and soul of a Christian? Surely there can be no genuine resurrection even of the soul if there is no real death."

My response is, "You are right. We must die physically and spiritually. But if I read the scriptures correctly (see Romans 8:1ff,

I Corinthians 15:1ff etal.) in Christ the Christian has already spiritually died and experienced the spiritual resurrection of new spiritual birth (See also John 3:1 etal.), and it is not necessary that he or she therein die still again." That is why it is not at all difficult to believe the Christian who says, "There is Jesus and He says that I am to come with Him. And I am glad." This one question alone is surely at the heart of the New Testament and worthy of books yet to be written.

I am grateful to the critic for raising still another issue: "But does the Bible not speak of death as sleep? Do the dead not simply fall asleep, not to awaken until Jesus physically returns to the earth to end the historical age and earth as we know it?"

My honest reply is, "Yes. That is true." The Bible, particularly the Old Testament, speaks of death as sleep most often based upon the belief that the soul cannot exist apart from the body. Ecclesiastes 3:19-20 is cited by various scholars as a classic example of this belief. These scholars rightly affirm that within this description of death as sleep, the fate of the sons of man and the fate of beasts is identical. As one dies, the other dies. The man has no advantage over other creatures. That is why the writer says, "All is vanity." All share the same destiny. All are from the dust of the earth and will return to dust.

Within the Old Testament Job also interprets death as a sleep, the soul being oblivious to anything apart from the body. "Why did I not die at birth?" he asked, "Why did I not come forth from the womb and expire? ... For then I would have lain down and been quiet. I should have slept..." (see Job 3:11ff).

Daniel, the Old Testament eschatological writer, expresses similar thought, but with the promise of a possible resurrection,

"And many of those who sleep in the dust of the earth shall awake, some to everlasting life, and some to everlasting life, and some to shame and everlasting contempt" (Daniel 12:20 RSV).

However, as all reputable commentaries on the Old Testament state in explaining this text, a resurrection is still predicated on the resurrection of the body. The soul cannot consciously exist apart from the body.

The New Testament, however, does not, based on my interpretation, "literally" hold to such an understanding. Rather, in The New Testament the term "sleep" is associated with death on several occasions, however, only as an earthly analogy or metaphor.

For example, the Apostle Paul said, "But we would not have you ignorant, brethren, concerning those who are asleep, that you may not grieve as others do who have no hope. For since we believe that Jesus died and rose again, even so, through Jesus, God will bring with Him those who have fallen asleep. For this we declare to you by the word of the Lord, that we who are alive who are left until the coming of the Lord, shall not precede those who have fallen asleep. For the Lord Himself will descend from heaven…then we who are alive, who are left, shall be caught up together with them in the clouds to meet the Lord in the air and so we shall always be with the Lord" (I Thessalonians 4:15-17 RSV).

However, this is the same Apostle Paul who said, "For to me to live is Christ, and to die is gain…I am hard pressed between the two. My desire is to depart (die) and be with Christ, for that is far better," (Philippians 1:21-23 RSV).

The Apostle Paul does use the metaphor of sleep. But, as many scholars rightly state, he also describes the soul as living outside the decaying physical body after death, not in a dead or comatose state, but fully cognizant and alive in communion with Jesus.

Most important to me is the fact that Jesus on occasion used the metaphor of sleep to describe death. Yet He said to the repentant thief crucified at His side, "Truly, I say to you, today you will be with Me in Paradise" (Luke 23:43, RSV). I am aware of the old punctuation argument that would call this interpretation into question, but I do not find it plausible. Jesus did not mean, "I am just talking to you today." That makes no sense to me, given that both Jesus and this repentant thief are experiencing death at the same time. Jesus meant that together they would be imminently in paradise following their death--only a breath away.

Further, it was Jesus Himself who used the metaphor of sleep in describing the death of his friend Lazarus. But when the disciples took the analogy literally, He corrected them saying, "No! Lazarus is dead" (see John 11:11ff). Jesus was simply trying to assist the disciples in their understanding. Sleep, although useful as a metaphor, is not to be equated with death.

It was Jesus who added still more clarity to the subject when He addressed the Sadducees and their questions regarding the law of Moses in response to death, marriage, and the resurrection. Jesus knew the Sadducees did not really believe in resurrection and were trying to confuse and discredit His person and ministry. Jesus immediately exposed their deceit, saying, " Now God (the God of Abraham, Isaac, and Jacob) is not the God of the dead, but of the living, for all (the living and the dead) live to Him." (Luke 20:38 RSV). Even the dead are alive.

The New Testament writer John in his Revelation (6:10) records that "they (in heaven) cried out in a loud voice, 'O Sovereign Lord, holy and true, how long before thou wilt judge… those who dwell upon the earth?" John might also ask the critic, "How could I have seen these souls in heaven very much alive crying out to God if they were simply asleep?"

Numerous other biblical images might be included here and merit discussion and reflection. Again, possibly another book. But my conclusion is this: sleep is a useful metaphor for the word "death," but it must not be taken too far. Then the idea of sleep creates more confusion than it assuages.

Death is not sleep. The dead are not unconscious. They are alive and they are awake. Christians are wonderfully aware that they are with Christ.

Now I have no doubt that the list of questions critics might ask are as numerous as the population of the world itself. After all, there is at least a little critic in all of us. But the four questions I have addressed here are the ones most often asked when discussing even with my closest friends the convictions I have shared in this book. I have found them to be especially important concerns among others who are in the process of grieving or anticipating their own death.

Perhaps simply to raise these questions; facilitating thought, prayer, and reflection; is alone worthy of the time and energy invested in this entire book.

If I had but one concluding prayer for us all, it would be this: Holy Father, May through your Son, Jesus Christ, we all be prepared to give an effective witness for You with only a moment's notice…and take the ultimate step without one! Amen.

APPENDIX A

The following abbreviations are used within the text of this book in reference to specific translations of the Bible.

KJV...The King James Version of the Bible, 1611.

RSV...The Revised Standard Version of the Bible, 1952.

NIV...The New International Version of the Bible, 1978.

APPENDIX B

The following references served as resources in the writing of this book. The list is not exhaustive, but affirms the historical data discussed.

Chapter 1

Ebert, Roger. "The Shootist." Roger Ebert.com. January 1, 1976. Access site: https://www.Rogerebert.com/review/the-shootist-1976.

Editors, Lom. "John Wayne Biography. The Biographer.com. April 22, 2017, updated September 11, 2019. Access site: https://www.biography.com/ actor/johnwayne.

Chapter 10

Buttrick, George. ed. *The Interpreter's Dictionary of the Bible.* "Death," Nashville: Abingdon Press, 1962.

Ibid. "Immorality."

Ibid. "Life"

Chase, Mitch. "Does the Old Testament Teach Resurrection Hope?" The Gospel Coalition. Access date: March 31, 2018. https:www.thegospelcoalition.org/article/old-testament-teach-ressurection-hope/

Craigie, Peter. *Word Biblical Commentary*, vol. 19, Psalms 1-50. "Psalms 23." Waco: Word Books, 1983.

CHAPTER 11

Beasely-Murray, George. *Word Biblical Commentary.* "John." Second edition, vol. 36. Nashville: Thomas Nelson Publishers, 1999.

Burge, Gary M. *The NIV Application Commentary.* "John." Grand Rapids: Zondervan Publishing House, 2000.

Hull, William. *The Broadman Bible Commentary.* "John." Nashville: Broadman Press, 1970.

Mills, Watson. ed. *Dictionary of the Bible.* Macon: Mercer University Press, 1990.

CHAPTER 12

Anderson, Bernhard. *Understanding of the Old Testament.* 3rd ed. Englewood Cliffs: Prentice Hill, Inc., 1975.

Buttrick, George, ed. *The Interpreter's Dictionary of the Bible.* "Hezekiah." Nashville: Abingdon Press, 1962.

Forbes, Wesley. ed. *The Baptist Hymnal.* Nashville, Convention Press, 1991.

Mills, Watson. ed. *Dictionary of the Bible.* Macon. Mercer University Press, 1990.

Paulien, Jon. "The Resurrection and the Old Testament: A Fresh Look in Light of Recent Research." *Journal of the Adventist Theological Society*, January, 2013.

Tabur, James. "What the Bible Really says About Death, Afterlife, and the Future (Part 1)." Taborlog: Religion Matters from the Bible to the Modern World. February 18, 2017.

Access site: https://www.jamestabor.com/what-the-bible-says-about-death-afterlife-and-the-future-part-1/

Todd, "Eternal Life in the Old Testament," Explore the Faith. January 4, 2019. Access site: https://www.explorethefaith.com/eternal-life-in-the-old-testament/

Wilson, Gerald. *The NIV Application Commentary*, vol. 1 "Psalms." Grand Rapids: Zondervan, 2002.

Chapter 13

Beasley-Murray, George. *Word Biblical Commentary.* "John." Second edition, vol. 36. Nashville: Thomas Nelson Publishers, 1999.

Botterweck and Ringgren. eds. Willis. Trans. *Theological Dictionary of the Old Testament.* Grand Rapids: William B. Eerdmans Publishing Co., 1970, 1971, 1972.

Brown, Colin. ed. *The New International Dictionary of the New Testament Theology.* Grand Rapids: Zondervan Publishing House, 1967, 1969, 1971.

Leicht, Brian. "Awake Beyond the Grave: What the Bible says about Soul Sleep." Insight for living Ministries. Article Library. July 16, 2013. Access site: https://www.insight.org/resources/article-library/individual/awake/beyond-the-grave-what-the-bible-says-about-soul-sleep.

Quotations

Bartlett, John. *Familiar Quotations.* Boston: Little, Brown and Company, 1950.

Kramer, Jade / Ascension Healing Therapies. "Grief and Mourning.com" Powered by WordPress.org. 2011-2018. Access site: https://www.griefandmourning.com/ quotes-about-death.